THANK YOU
FOR THE DAYS

ABOUT THE AUTHOR

Deirdre Brady was born into the O'Faolain family in Dublin in 1942. She left school at fifteen, and married at twenty.

A mother of seven, throughout the years Deirdre has been writing distinct vignettes about her life. This is her first book.

She lives in Dublin with her husband, Eamon.

THANK YOU
FOR THE DAYS

DEIRDRE BRADY

**TOWN
HOUSE**
DUBLIN

First published in 2005 by

TownHouse, Dublin
THCH Ltd
Trinity House
Charleston Road
Ranelagh
Dublin 6
Ireland

www.townhouse.ie

1 2 3 4 5 6 7 8 9 10

ISBN: 1-86059-240-6

Cover design by Sin É Design
Text design and typeset by Sin É Design
Printed and bound by
Nørhaven Paperback A/S, Denmark

For Don, Ronán and Dermot, who have gone before us,
and for my dear grandchildren, whose lives are ahead of them.

ACKNOWLEDGEMENTS

This book would not have come about without the help of the following: my dear son, Ciarán, who is responsible for the genesis of this book; Wayne, my favourite (and only) son-in-law, who was tenacious in his encouragement; Eamon, my best friend, spelling-checker, dinner-maker and critic; my children, Eoin, who gave me a computer; Máireád, Clare, Dónal and Paraic, who, in turn, patiently taught me how to use it; kind sister Nuala, for her blessing and her cheering phone calls; daughters-in-law, sisters and brother, for their support; Trudi and Cailín for their quirky comments; TownHouse publishers for their expertise and guidance; my old friend Margaret Dolan, who advised me in my early writing; and my unique English teacher, Síle Fitzgerald, who believed that I could.

A wide driveway curves from the gate lodge, across the field at the rear of our house, to our landlord's Georgian mansion. Tall trees overshadow each side of the driveway, a profusion of daffodils beneath their shelter.

I decide to pick a bunch for Mammy. Arms laden with flowers, I look up to see the landlord's wife standing above me.

'Why did you take those without permission?' She demands in a stern voice. Flushed with guilt, I am too frightened to speak. As I straighten up, I feel warm liquid trickle down my legs. A dark puddle spreads on the ground around my soppy shoes.

I lay the yellow blooms on the grass beneath a tree, then turn and squelch home, as fast as my thumping heart allows.

BEGINNINGS

On 5 February 1942, my mother was reading a biography of Queen Victoria when she went into labour with me, her third child. At the time she was living on the Cabra Road, alone with two little toddlers. Dad was away – on duty as an officer in the army.

Mam didn't panic or fuss. She had had easy deliveries with the others. She walked to the nearest telephone booth and rang her father, who lived a few miles away. He duly arrived to mind the small fry, and gave her the money for a taxi to the Rotunda Hospital. She read her book between contractions, and when she was told 'Congratulations, you have a healthy baby girl', she groaned with disappointment, picked up her open book, and said, 'Oh no, are you sure? Look again!'

Now they had three daughters: Gráinne, Nuala, and me. Dad had wished for a son, and she wanted to please him. Mam told us this story many times over the years – much to my embarrassment. Two years before my ignoble entrance into this world, the family had been renting the west wing of an old rambling mansion known as Boley in Monkstown, County Dublin. Gráinne was born there in 1938 – in the billiard room. Mam and Dad had put a double mattress on top of some old tea chests, and their landlord, a Sir Valentine Grace, was invited in to see the new baby. A huge, corpulent gentleman, he seated his massive weight on the bottom corner of the bed, instantly propelling mother and child up in the air. Dad, who had been standing at the top of the bed, expertly caught little Gráinne.

So Mammy told us.

Boley was haunted by the ghost of an elegant old lady, believed to be Lady Grace, who had died at the turn of the last century. She wafted through empty, bare rooms in a long black dress.

On one occasion, Granda – a solid, sensible Kerryman – stayed overnight. The next morning at breakfast, he told of how he had been woken up in the dead of night by the silent figure of an old lady standing beside his bed. Mam and Dad had forgotten to tell him about the ghost. They just accepted her.

Years later, Mam recounted dreamily, 'Sometimes your father would arrive home in the afternoon. I would put little Gráinne down for a nap, and put baby Nuala out in her pram under the huge tree. Then we would make love.'

The bill had to be paid before leaving the Rotunda, so Granda came up trumps again and paid for me. I think I was always a favourite of his from then on. One of my earliest memories is of being perched on his knee whilst he bobbed me up and down, singing, 'Who's the flower of the flock, who's the queen of the garden, who's the flower of the flock, who's my little darling?'

Granda was a tall, lean, quiet man. Dark haired, with bushy eyebrows, he came from Kerry to Dublin with his bride in 1915. They rented a largish redbrick house in Clonliffe Road. Granda worked as a lowly clerk in the General Post Office, while his wife, Marion, worked from home as a tailoress, in between raising a large family. She died suddenly, aged just forty-five. A photograph shows a woman with huge, dark, deep-set eyes, and thick, black, wavy hair. By all accounts, she was a fiery little lady who ruled the household.

My mother, Catherine, inherited her luxurious hair and her explosive temper. As a young woman, Mam was shy and bookish. She had a firm, rounded, curvy figure, soft uncreased skin and even, white teeth. And a beautiful smile. She was introduced to Tomás O'Faolain on a foursome blind date in a dancehall called the Swiss Chalet in Dublin City.

Mam was then a gauche girl of eighteen. Dad was five years older, confident and urbane, with a degree from UCD. He had been the editor of the college magazine, and was teaching English in a school in Blackrock. Mam had done her Leaving Cert through Irish and was working in a library – her first and only job. They discovered that they both loved their native language, that he too lived in Clonliffe Road and, according to Mam, 'It was love at first sight. We sat on the stairs and talked and talked. We forgot all about our two friends. He walked me home in the early hours. My father was furious. I didn't care. I was floating!'

As a young man, Dad was slim, fit and vigorous, not very tall, but always impeccably dressed. His thin, long face was crowned with a pronounced widow's peak of fine, black hair. He had grey-blue eyes to Mam's green eyes, and perfectly groomed hands in comparison to Mam's short, stubby ones. His clear, clipped, light-hearted voice was probably his best asset.

Mam was a virgin before she met him, and her sexual awakening was wonderful and shameless. Listening to her reminisce years later, it seemed as if their physical love had endured throughout all their turbulent years together. He was to be her first and only love.

In the 1930s in Ireland, both the Church and society frowned heavily on a pregnant young bride-to-be, and Mam and Dad had to get married at six o'clock in the morning. They were not allowed a nuptial mass – just a simple ceremony.

Not that they felt any shame: they weren't much interested in religion or convention.

'It was a cold, dark, January morning,' Mam told us. 'I wore a dark blue costume, and your father looked so handsome in his new suit. His parents laid on a wedding breakfast – a real one. We had bacon and eggs and brown bread. Then we got a lift to the boat for Holyhead. We stayed in a small hotel in the heart of London. Don't ask me anything about it though, as we hardly left our room for the whole week.'

MOVING ON

After Boley, Mam, Dad and my two elder sisters lived in a cottage in the wilds of Donegal.

When World War II began, Dad joined the Irish army. As an officer during the 'Emergency', as Ireland liked to call it, his growing family moved house quite often.

'My assignment was of the utmost importance – for our people and our country,' he informed us gravely. But there was a hint of a smile in his voice!

'Every morning, your mother would hand me my lunch and a clean white handkerchief. Dressed in full uniform, I would set off on my bike for the windy lookout post, perched on top of a cliff. Carefully unfolding my hanky, I would vigorously polish the glass of the huge telescope, then scan the grey, blank sea for an enemy submarine or battleship. As the weeks dragged by, cold and bleary-eyed, I began to wish for the sight of a periscope attempting to invade our neutral waters.'

From Donegal, the family moved back to Dublin; first to Cabra Road and then to a rented cottage called Black Linn at the top of Howth Hill.

When Dad was posted to the Curragh, they settled in what was to be their longest stay – eight years – in the countryside surrounding Malahide in County Dublin. Home was an isolated bungalow, a good mile up the hill from the village. It was called Little Broomfield, in deference to the grander Georgian house of our landlord, Broomfield. We could glimpse it across the fields, concealed behind tall trees.

My brother Terry was born at home, on a balmy July night. Dad had his son and heir at last, so he cracked open a bottle of whiskey he had been saving, and he stayed up celebrating with Doctor Michael from the village. We girls were allowed in to see the baby next morning. Mam glowed with happiness, sitting up in the pink satin-quilted bed, a ribbon tied around her long, thick hair, her little son tucked in beside her.

Once out of babyhood, little Terry didn't get any more attention than the rest of us. Dad and books came first with Mammy.

Mammy came from strong Kerry stock. Childbearing came naturally to her. No notion of family planning. Thirteen pregnancies throughout the years, nine children altogether. When we lived in Malahide, there were five children with only about two years between any of us.

Gráinne was the eldest. She was neat and pretty with fine, black hair and a beautiful singing voice. Everyone agreed she looked just like the child film star, Elizabeth Taylor.

Nuala, two years younger, was clever and bossy. She had wild curly hair and dressed like a tomboy. She was our leader, and instigated most of our adventures. Nuala was always reading – just like Mammy – anything she could find: adult books, comics, library books. She got bored with us easily. Two years her junior, I accepted unquestionably that Nuala knew everything!

Terry, next to me in age, was a thin, quiet, shy boy. He wore a serious expression, a puzzled kind of frown, until it was discovered that he had a squint in one eye and he had to get spectacles. These ended up in bits, quite regularly, as Terry confided to me how he loved being brought into the city for new ones. 'Mammy always treated me to Woolworths afterwards for lunch.'

I was closer to Terry, as Nuala and Gráinne were always paired together. They were sent to ballet lessons, and even horse-riding lessons, for a while.

Don, or Donald as he was christened, was the blue-eyed, curly-mopped toddler. He was a handsome, chubby little chap, with eyelashes you could sweep the floor with. He trailed round after us, bubbly and good-humoured. Once, Terry got into trouble for cutting off some of Don's curls with Mammy's scissors.

I had straight, brown hair, mostly clipped to one side, a biggish nose, but nice green eyes. I was not much interested in grown-ups, or life outside our home. I think I was quite stubborn, but I was happy most of the time. I liked to play house, making mud pies and being the mammy to my younger brothers. I always fell in with my big sisters' plans, and was quite biddable.

Before we attended Malahide National School, we three eldest girls were sent to a private pre-school in a big old house down the hill.

All I can recall from that time is the food (I must have been a hungry little girl), the big apple in my bag and the grandfather clock on the landing.

Waiting for midday: lunchtime.

CHILDLIFE

Although it was only two miles each way to Malahide and Portmarnock, my brothers and sisters and I were cocooned in our own little world, with each other for playmates, and the fields, forest and railway tracks as our playground.

Our bungalow was snugly surrounded by fields. The distant rumbling of an approaching steam train was a signal to race across the spongy grass and to scream and shout excitedly against its heavy puff-puff. We waited for its smoke to envelop us as it chugged past laboriously.

Sometimes, between trains, we'd place big pennies on the shiny tracks, retrieving them later, thinner and flattened. Or we'd walk along the wooden sleepers to rob an orchard, climbing down from the railway via strong, pear-tree branches. Then, stuffing our knickers with apples, we'd scale back up again, terrified the owner's dogs might have picked up our scent.

In high summer we had lots of picnics, sometimes just outside the kitchen door. Mam would spread a blanket on the grass for us, then bring out a huge salad platter, cups, and a bottle of lemonade. For more exotic locations – Malahide or Portmarnock Strand – Mam and Dad carried the youngest on their bicycles, and the family cycled in single file along the lush country lanes.

We constructed secret hideaways near our home, by building a roof of branches over mossy ditches. Bottles of water, comics and biscuits were sneaked in. Huddled together, we held important private meetings in whispers, safe from detection by the occasional passer-by.

When our landlord piled gigantic squares of hay in one of his fields, we would climb through the dark spaces, hiding from each other. At teatime, our hair and clothes sprouted hayseed.

Trumbles' Woods, as we called it – a wild overgrown demesne – was our private territory. We picked loganberries from its tangled orchard, whilst the eerie cry of magnificent peacocks and peahens echoed through the wood. In autumn, its mossy banks yielded up treasures of nuts and cones.

When winter evenings forced us in, I had a scrapbook to stick pretty pictures into, and Terry had his stamp collection to keep him busy. A more robust activity was a game we all played with the long, wooden kitchen table. One end was propped high up on kitchen chairs, a quilt placed on the floor, and then we took turns sliding down its steep incline.

One crisp, icy moonlit night the field next to us, which had been flooded, froze over with strong, thick ice. We skated, slid and ran across it in our old shoes. Children from far down the road joined us and the night air was punctured by our excited cries.

BURIED TREASURE

'If you want to come on the "mitch" with us, you'll have to do what we tell you.'

Gráinne and Nuala were perched on top of the gate at the end of our driveway, waiting for me.

'What's a "mitch"?'

'It's not an anything. It just means we're going to pretend to go to school. But instead we are really going swimming. It's roasting hot today.'

'But we've no togs!'

'Of course not, silly. We can swim in our knickers. There'll be hardly anyone on the beach on Monday morning. Are you coming or not?'

I had to think it out, but they jumped down off the gate and walked on up the leafy road without me.

'Wait for me!' I caught up with them.

'All right, I'll come with you.'

I was sticky, hot and flustered, and the thought of the cool sea smothered my little worries.

Instead of turning left at the crossroads in the village for the gloomy, redbrick schoolhouse, we sneaked to the right, along by the Malahide seafront.

The girls decided on a suitably private stretch of beach, just before the rocky merging with Portmarnock. We whooped with delight as we flopped down onto our empty kingdom of warm sand.

'Now, Deirdre, the first thing we all have to do is to bury our schoolbags, sandals and clothes. Nothing must give us away while we're in the water.'

We stripped to our navy cotton knickers. This was so exciting. I couldn't wait to race into the sea. But firstly, I dug a deep hole with my hands, then carefully placed my things on top of each other. I piled back the sand, arms flying, until there was only a slight mound.

I searched around for a marker. Ah! A seagull's feather. I stuck it upright, bang in the centre of my bump, then abandoned my skinny six-year-old body to the delights of the sparkling sea.

The two girls hopped past me out to deeper water. I couldn't swim yet, so I raced up and down the edge, flinging myself on my tummy every now and then, kicking my legs, and shouting to my sisters in my happiness.

This was heaven. Who cared about horrible school on a perfect June morning?

Later we made a sandcastle, with a moat and a channel for the incoming tide to creep up. We decorated it with beautiful shells, and then we had another swim.

It was decided that we'd have our picnic as soon as the Angelus bells rang out from the distant church spire. Our school lunch would do nicely. My tummy was hollow from hunger. Hurry up bells.

At last we heard their welcome bong. Hooray. Thank you, Holy Mary, thank you.

Our sandy bodies scattered like arrows to dig up our schoolbags.

Where was my spot? My seagull's feather? Every mound I pounced upon looked just like it. I dug hole after hole. There were feathers all over the sand. I couldn't find my pile anywhere. Crying, I ran back along the beach to the girls. They were starting their jam sandwiches.

'You silly baby,' eight-year-old Nuala shouted. 'We'll all be in trouble now. All because of you. Just wait till Mammy sees you. And stop whinging!'

But they helped me search wildly, and when we gave up, they shared their lunch with me.

Barefoot and red-faced, in my shabby knickers, I trailed home behind my sisters. Through the village of Malahide, and all the way up the hill, I kept my head down to avoid the stares of passers-by, while my tears splashed on my toes and the path.

Mammy was sitting out in a deckchair, book in hand, as curly-haired toddler Don played at her feet. She wore a straw hat and a gay, flowery dress.

My sisters disappeared into the house.

Mam looked at me in silence for a minute, then held out her arms. Lifting me onto her lap, she dried my tears as I poured out my tale of woe.

Next day, back at school, our names were called out. One by one we approached the teacher's desk at the top of the class, and held out our hands for a whack of the ruler. The children giggled and tittered as we returned to our seats. They'd heard all about our 'day off'.

Curiously, I didn't mind too much. I knew my Mammy loved me.

OUT THE ROAD

Now that I was seven and a half, it was time for my first far journey, away from home.

I was to accompany Nuala and Gráinne on the four-mile walk to and from Baldoyle School.

They would mind me.

But they never waited for me.

As I dallied and daydreamed along, leisurely pulling a feathery fern that stretched out from the ditch at the side of the road, I glimpsed their skinny satchelled figures far ahead.

It seemed an endless, solitary trek. Only the caw-caw of the rooks and the squelch of my shoes for company.

And I didn't heave a sigh of relief on reaching school at last.

Hunger pervaded my thoughts and body as morning classes trudged onwards. I yearned for the lunch bell to clang, so that I could devour my bread and jam sandwiches and my bottle of slightly sour milk.

The return journey was a lighter, gayer trip. Each step brought me nearer to Mammy and the warm kitchen. I yearned for the taste of the delicious lump of fresh bread I would tear from the heart of the loaf.

A clean, blue, sunny May morning. This day for me alone. My First Holy Communion.

The white cotton dress both my sisters had worn, freshly starched and ironed. The short gauzy veil, with a circle of tiny crushed rosebuds on the headband.

As Mammy clips it securely into my shining brushed hair, I draw on the rolled soft gloves, and slip the strap of the rich, leather handbag up to my elbow.

Hand in hand, we contentedly walk the bare mile to the church, my excitement and happiness binding us together.

I savour the snug feel of my ankle socks and watch in mute admiration as my feet lift one brand-new sandal in front of the other.

THE MERRIEST CHRISTMAS

Christmas 1950. Dad had a whole week off, so his first important task was to choose a tree. All five of us children marched along to keep in step with him, as we set off for nearby Trumbles' Woods, Dad with a huge, heavy axe on his shoulder.

Having selected a handsome specimen, Dad proceeded to chop it down, while we collected cones and holly. Back home that evening, we painted the cones silver, then hung them alongside our homemade crêpe paper decorations.

On Christmas Eve, we sent up our letters to Santa via the huge log fire. We asked for small surprises – just like every other year. We hung no stockings on our beds; we had never heard of the custom.

On Christmas morning, we dressed in our best Sunday clothes, with new mittens and pixies. Rosy-cheeked and shiny, the family set off at a brisk pace, walking crocodile fashion down the bare-hedged country road. We were going to Mass down in Malahide Village. We always wished baby Jesus a happy birthday first. It was only good manners.

Afterwards, we skipped impatiently all the way home, calling back to Mam and Dad to hurry up, barely able to contain our excitement.

Within minutes of arriving home, the entire family queued up outside the sitting room door, youngest first.

This year, it was little Don's turn. With Dad's help, the key was put in the lock beneath the brown wooden handle. Don's pudgy little hands seemed to take ages to turn it. Suddenly the door burst open and we all tumbled in, the piny smell of the freshly cut Christmas tree filling our senses. Shrieks of delight and surprise filled the room as each child found their presents.

Over by the square bay window stood a sky-blue boy's bicycle, bare and gleaming. A white page was stuck to the silver handlebars, and written starkly in big red letters was my name, DEIRDRE. I thought my breathing had stopped as I stood uncertainly in front of this shining dream and painstakingly read the words.

'Deirdre, I know you are a good and kind girl. I have given you a boy's bike so that you can bring your little brother Don to school on the crossbar. Love Santa.'

Bursting with pride and happiness I tore off the note and rushed over to Dad.

'Look! Santa has given me a brand-new bicycle. A boy's one. And he spelt my name properly.'

He patted my head and smiled, understanding perfectly.

I sat on the floor to admire my sparkling machine. My first ever. I couldn't even cycle. But I would learn in time for school. It was hard to believe that it was really all mine.

I was so used to being overlooked at home. I didn't mind at all. It seemed quite reasonable. Gráinne, the eldest at twelve, was the beauty; Nuala, the clever one; Terry was the first-born son and heir; and Don was cute and funny. I thought I was plain and quiet.

But this very Christmas, Santa had singled me out from the others, and given me the best present of all.

STEPPING OUT

On lonely winter evenings, Mam often sent me down to the village library on my new bicycle to exchange her books.

My bike had no lamp, so my return journey was a challenge. The streetlights stopped at the top of the hill and I had to cycle into the enveloping blackness as their glow faded behind me. My only guide was the dusky ribbon of sky above the dark, menacing trees. Eyes scrunched with strain, I whistled and pedalled furiously, my cold hands gripping the handlebars tight with the terror of the night.

Dad believed in instilling courage and self-reliance into us girls. When we were twelve, ten, and eight respectively, we were allowed to do our Christmas shopping in Woolworths in Dublin City.

But firstly, we had the exciting ceremony of our red pillar money boxes being opened and counted by him. There were cheers as he announced, 'Gráinne has saved three pounds this year. Well done! Nuala has managed to reach the grand sum of two pounds and ten shillings. And Deirdre has done well, with twelve shillings and six pence saved.'

Before leaving us at Nelson's Pillar, Dad asked me to repeat my name and address twice.

'And what do we do if we get lost?' he prompted.

'Find a policeman and tell him where I live.'

As he disappeared down O'Connell Street, amongst the crowd of big, big people, and my sisters crossed the wide road ahead of me, I decided I was lost almost at once.

I calmly followed instructions, and was returned home safely to Little Broomfield in the back of a black police motorcar.

Swimming too was another test. Dad taught us the 'dead man's float', and after that it was up to ourselves. I was still practising the doggie paddle in the shallow end when I was eleven! My sisters and their friends swam at the end of the slip in deep water.

Every day I promised I'd join them.

'I can swim now,' I'd boast, but I was scared.

The day I finally walked the length of the slip, Nuala pushed me into the sea below.

'Now,' she called down. 'Either swim over to the ladder, or sink!'

I managed to doggie paddle to safety. Everyone cheered as I climbed back up. I'm still grateful for that 'encouragement'!

Across the road from us was the gateway to McDowells' farm. Mam would send me up their long driveway to get milk from their dairy.

The thin wire handle of the billycan cut into my hand as I carried it home. Taking a rest, I'd admire the handsome horses the Mc Dowells trained in a fenced-off field. When their horse Caughoo won the Grand National, there were great celebrations and free drink in Malahide Village.

Once a year at Christmas time, we visited Dad's family in Clonliffe Road. His mother – a demure, plump, smiling old lady – would have all sorts of treats for us children. She wore black lacy Victorian dresses, and her snowy white hair was pinned neatly in waves. Granda Phelan had joined the British Army during World

War I, so that he could send home a good wage each week. I was told that he was invalided home, with a piece of shrapnel still imbedded in him. Later he took up a more gentle occupation in Williams and Woods, and brought home the most sumptuous confectionery and sweets.

My aunt Anne, Dad's sister, was our host. She worked as a supervisor in the Irish Sweepstakes office in Ballsbridge. She was petite, always beautifully dressed, with thick, black, curly hair. Eyes screwed half shut against the smoke from the cigarette stuck at the side of her mouth, Anne weaved around the sitting room, giving each of us an orange and a chocolate, cheerily chatting away at the same time.

One particular year, Nuala produced *The Mad Hatter's Tea Party*. All four of us starred, squashed around a table at the end of their dark hall. Don was the dormouse, as he loved naps, and I got the important role of Alice.

On special occasions back home, Nuala and Gráinne would perform a short extract from *Swan Lake*. Dad would lower the needle gently onto the record as each emerged from behind the long curtains in front of the French windows. With very serious faces, they would bounce, dip and pirouette on tippy-toes.

When they had finished bowing several times, they would move close together and sing 'All in an April Evening' in earnest harmony. Whilst Gráinne would soar lightly up to the top notes, Nuala would labour breathlessly in seconds, an octave below.

Sometimes Gráinne would sing 'Deep in my heart, there's a little brown bird singing'. I felt a little sad and uncomfortable to think of the poor tiny bird trapped inside Gráinne's heart!

A COLOURFUL AFTERNOON

Yippee! We girls were in charge. Minding the house and the youngsters. Mam and Dad were gone into town. They wouldn't be back for hours.

Gráinne's friend Margaret and her little brother Joey came across the fields to play with us.

So what would we do today?

'I know,' Nuala decided. She always came up with original ideas. 'We'll give Daddy a nice surprise. We'll paint the garage doors for him.'

'Yeah!' We chorused excitedly, tumbling after her into the shadowy garage.

Dad kept all his paints and brushes neatly on a shelf there. I held a stool for Terry, as he awkwardly passed tins and jars down to us.

We decided on bright, shiny red, but two-and-a-half-year-old Joey started bawling, so we gave him a sealed tin of green paint and a stick to bang it with, to keep him happy.

The rest of us were allotted a position each in front of the huge, peeling wooden doors: Nuala, Gráinne and Margaret were on chairs to reach the higher spots. We were puffed with pride at our clever system.

One hour later, the scene was a rainbow of utter chaos. My jam jar of paint was very tacky, so I added water to it. It wouldn't spread on the wood, but dripped generously onto my shoes and socks. Gráinne tried to reach the top of the doors, and dropped her brush – laden with red paint – on five-year-old Don's head. Joey, meanwhile, was sitting in a puddle of green paint, happily banging on the upturned tin.

Nuala and Margaret lashed away vigorously. They had two thirds of one garage door patchily stuck with bright crimson when the paint ran out.

Hands, clothes, pebbles on the path, were all sploshed with colour. Of course we didn't know that gloss paint need turpentine. Suddenly, Margaret's voice rang out.

'Oh, look at Joey! I'll be killed.'

We all turned to look at Joey. He had decided that a slob of green on the door was enchanting. Having dispensed with his stick, he was using his fat little hands instead.

'Don't worry. We'll give him a bath,' Gráinne suggested. So we all traipsed into the bathroom to observe the proceedings. The water was freezing, and no amount of scrubbing with sunlight soap seemed to erase the paint from the shivering, bawling little chap. Yet the bath was a riot of red and green smudges.

Terry's streaked face appeared round the doorway. 'Quick, Mammy and Daddy are coming up the drive!'

Leaving Joey's sticky clothes on the bathroom floor, Margaret lifted him out of the bath, took his hand, and raced out the back door, heading for home across the fields. We watched his roundy white bottom bounce through the grass – the only paint-free part of him.

Dad looked very serious.

'Daughters. I want to speak to you. In your bedroom.'

I stayed where I was as Nuala and Gráinne followed him. He paused.

'Deirdre. What age are you now?'

'I'll be nine next February,' I said, proudly.

'Good. You're old enough to take responsibility too.'

Our punishment was to stay in our bedroom for the rest of the day. With no dinner.

As I sobbed into my pillow, yearning for the bright sunshine outside my window, I chastised myself.

Why didn't I say I was only eight?

FAIRY-TALE WORLD

During our years in Malahide, Mam was as good a mother as she knew how. Although we were as poor as church mice, we children didn't know this, as we had no neighbours. Mam was young, healthy, and very much in love with Dad, as he was with her. Sometimes they spoke endearments to each other in Irish so that us youngsters wouldn't understand.

Every Monday morning at dawn, Dad set off on his trusty bike for the thirty-eight-mile journey to distant, misty Kildare. We wouldn't see him again until Friday evening when, strong, smiling and healthy, he would unload his basket of fresh vegetables, grown in the fertile soil of the Curragh army camp!

At home in Little Broomfield, Dad liked to garden. He talked about plants as though they were people. 'I think this fellow needs a drink,' or 'Those roses look hungry; let's feed them.'

He grew tomatoes in the greenhouse adjoining the long

veranda at the front of the bungalow. Down the steps to the garden, directly facing the house, he planted a huge circular bed of flowers. Wallflowers in spring; roses in summer.

Behind the house was a tangled, neglected quarter acre of thick long grass, weed and meadow. Dad cleared a patch with his scythe, and encouraged me to sow parsley seeds there. 'This is your responsibility now.'

I watered and weeded for an eternity, until I was rewarded as little shoots of parsley pushed up through the clay.

When Dad was in the army, my job was to brasso the buttons of his uniform until 'you can see your face in them'. A threepenny bit was my pay. My first ever major purchase was in the local shop, where Mammy sent us with her ration book during the 'Emergency'. I bought five woodbine cigarettes for Dad's birthday present with my earnings!

Mammy didn't drink or smoke then, even though Dad was away a lot – first in the Curragh, and afterwards with the Irish Tourist Board. They seemed just perfect to me, safe in my blinkered childhood.

Throughout those lean rationing years, Mam fed us bully-beef stew, fried bread and dripping, rabbit casserole, porridge, and delicious apple dumplings.

We were dosed with castor oil and syrup of figs every Saturday night, and were a healthy, unkempt bunch.

Mam washed our clothes with sunlight soap on a scrubbing board in the bath, and blackleaded the kitchen range occasionally, but otherwise she wasn't bothered with housework. Reading her book was more urgent.

On winter evenings, in front of a roaring log fire, I would squeeze behind her armchair and brush her long tresses while she read. One night in particular, as I peered over her shoulder to examine one whole page of unintelligible words, I was worried. I had just achieved a proud moment in school – I could finally count up to the enormous amount of one hundred! I knew that there were much more than one hundred letters on that page. How would I ever learn all those words, so that I too could read a book?

In summertime, the countryside was an unending source of important things for us children to do. There was a long driveway down to our front gate. Halfway down, a huge ash tree stretched its strong branches high above a dark pond, blocked from the sun by bamboo canes and bushes. Dad hung a grand swing there– complete with wooden seat and scarlet ropes. What wonderful terror it was to fly out and back, over the black water below, clinging onto the ropes for dear life!

Water hens and their young slipped across the pond's surface, and its soppy, mucky banks were a rich source of tadpoles. Deciding to explore the centre of the pond's dark, murky depths one parentless day, we dragged the heavy lid of a trunk down to the edge, and flipped it over. It would do nicely as a one-man boat. As the skinniest, Terry was elected. He set sail for the middle of the pond, a branch doubling as an oar, while we cheered him on.

Halfway across, the trunk began to sink slowly, then disappeared. His white legs plastered in mud up to his knees, red-faced Terry paddled back to the bank. We all stood, silent and defeated, staring at the spot where our ship had vanished.

There was a succession of pet dogs in Malahide, but our

favourite was a shaggy terrier named Nelly. She ran wild with us through ditches, fields and forest. On school days, Nelly raced down the drive to greet us, tail wagging hysterically.

One afternoon, on arriving home, there was no sign of her. Mammy told us she was missing. We found her, dead, inside a gateway up the road. She had eaten poisoned meat which had been laid down in a field. We lifted her in silence, and carried her stiff, straight body home. We dug a grave beside the pond, and buried Nelly there. A cross made from twigs marked the spot.

That was a heavy, bleak night in our home, as each of us cried quietly in our beds.

A long time after, some child suggested digging up the grave – to see how Nelly was. There was no sign of our dog – just hundreds of squirming, tiny, white worms. A horrible ditty that was popular then reminded me of Nelly: 'The worms crawl in, and the worms crawl out, they crawl in thin, and they come out stout!'

***

Walking home from the village with my two sisters one chilly November afternoon, I chattered on about Christmas and what I hoped Santa would bring me.

As we topped the brow of the hill, Nuala turned around impatiently. 'Don't tell me you still believe in Santa. You know it's Mammy and Daddy who buy the presents.'

In shock and dismay, I looked imploringly at Gráinne.

'Yes, it's true, Deirdre. You are too old to believe in fairy-tales,' she said in her 'no-nonsense' tone of voice.

The two of them sighed with importance and grown-up-ness,

then turned and marched on ahead of me.

The deep pain in my tummy increased as I pondered this terrible revelation. I knew it must be true. My blue boy's bike, my lovely doll that had to go to the dolls' hospital when its face got broken. Mammy and Daddy had given them to me really. It made sense.

But I was not ready to be enlightened. I mourned for the loss of my wonderful Santa.

Too old at nine.

*****

After a break of nearly five years, Mam brought home a new baby girl from hospital in 1950. Fair-skinned and baldy, with huge, blue eyes, she was christened Noreen, after Mam's youngest sister. Aunt Noreen had been nursing in London when she contracted tuberculosis. She knew there was no cure, and so came home in 1942. She died, aged just twenty-one, in the Pigeon House – a dark, narrow sanatorium at the end of Ringsend Pier.

Less than two years later, baby Marian joined us, a placid, dark-haired, plump infant. So now there were seven.

Daddy was moving up and out into the world. His distinctive voice was now being heard on Radio Éireann, and his weekly *Musical Quiz* proved very popular throughout Ireland. This programme was Mammy's brainchild, but there was no place for her and she couldn't do anything about it.

We left Malahide for good, suddenly one summer's night, squashed amongst our belongings in the back of a motorcar. I thought it was very exciting. Why so suddenly? Perhaps there was some rent owed.

We lived in Laytown, a seaside town, for a few months, and then moved to Balbriggan. Alone with us most of the time, Mam took to going up to Dublin every Thursday. She started to smoke, and began to take a drink or two.

LARAGH DAYS

Late one summer's night we moved into Laragh House – a large crumbling three-storey Victorian building – on the corner of Church Street and Skerries Street in Balbriggan.

On the street side, the front door, which was never used, led into the main hall through a gloomy, neglected conservatory. Inside and out, the glass was coated with years of grime. None of us ever went in there. We always used the tall, pillared doorway at the side of the house. Opposite this doorway, a huge, tangled garden was resplendently choked with apple trees and rose bushes, a laburnum tree and a majestic weeping willow. The neglected garden was a challenge to Dad, and a mysterious jungle to us children.

We raced all over the house 'bagsing' our own rooms. Gráinne choose the nicest room on the second floor. Nuala moved into a small room beside the side porch that was eventually christened the 'mouse room' because the mice rather fancied it. It was also handy for sneaking out of the house for romantic trysts!

I picked a room on the top floor. I had to bring a candle on a saucer up there at night as the house had gas lighting on the first two floors only. The delicate white gas wicks broke easily and there was never much hurry to replace them, so the whole house was a mishmash of darkness and light at night-time.

The room next to mine became the 'apple room', where Dad stored his crop each autumn – making sure that no two apples touched each other. The aroma of ripe fruit was overpoweringly delicious whenever the door was opened.

There was also a secret garden that was accessible only by climbing out of the drawing room windows. At Halloween, Dad tied masses of fireworks to the branches of an old tree there, and we all wiggled out to watch the magical explosions of colour shoot dizzily up into the navy sky.

Rose, our maid, had moved with us from Malahide. Considering how poor we were financially, it seems strange now to have had a maid, but it was the norm then, and she was considered part of the family.

I remember one winter when all of us, including Rose, had the measles. Mam instructed Gráinne, who was well, to put a level teaspoon of salt into a pot of steeping porridge. Next morning, our startled taste buds quickly discovered that she had stirred in eleven spoonfuls!

I never went to Rose's room, only as far as the door, to give her her weekly romantic magazines, *Oracle* and *Miracle*.

Dad was now a newspaper journalist and had taken Granda's name – Terry O'Sullivan – as his pen name. He was given a distinctive two-toned Consul car and a photographer, and was driving all over the country, writing a weekly page for the *Sunday Press*. He looked the picture of prosperity.

Yet back home, Mam mightn't have one and sixpence to give me for school stockings. Neither of them was mean. They were just hopeless money managers.

There was great fuss when Dad was sent to New York by his newspaper. The *Press* couldn't afford to send a photographer as well, so lots of pictures were taken before he left Dublin: Dad in a Frank Sinatra – type hat, long coat and pipe (he didn't smoke one), in various poses – looking up, hailing a cab. These were then superimposed against a New York setting for publication back in Ireland.

He brought back super presents for all of us: an evening top encrusted with jet-black beads for Mammy, a white satin blouse for me.

So Dad was off, mixing with the rich and want-to-be famous people, while Mam was stuck in the chaos of our bare home in Balbriggan – only the drawing room was properly furnished – with seven children to mind.

My sisters and I attended the local convent. It was mainly for boarders, and we day girls were looked down upon. I found sixth class tough, academically, but I worked hard and made myself do my homework the minute I got home, on an old table and chair plonked on one side of the large, square hall.

I loved drama, and the elocution teacher worked hard to help rid me of my pronounced lisp. I was good at athletics and, at the end of the year, I was presented with a navy plastic case of Basildon Bond stationery – for a first in athletics. I was so proud – the first thing I'd ever won! I kept it for years and years.

I was always untidy and dishevelled, missing a button, or with my stockings falling down. I often had to ask Mam for a sixpence to replace the stud on my suspender belt. She would give out stink. 'I want that back this afternoon!'

A button might have to suffice the next day. I walked around the school in dread of it popping out onto the floor. This happened frequently, which meant I would have one suspender tentatively holding up my stocking until I reached home.

In autumn I packed my schoolbag with apples and sold them to the boarders at lunchtime for two pence each. To balance this shady practice, I would climb to the top of the high brick wall separating our wild garden from the Sunshine Home – pockets bulging with fruit – and throw apples down to the inner city children who were treated to a seaside holiday there.

I made my Confirmation in Balbriggan with my brother Terry. Mam dressed us in identical grey wool suits – except mine had a skirt. The lady in the Silk Mills shop in Dublin said to my mother as I paraded up and down, 'Such a lovely figure! She could be a model.'

At school we were encouraged to read the life of the saint whose name we had picked for Confirmation. Up in my turret, I read a book about St Rose of Lima – a fourteen-year-old girl who'd been martyred for her faith. At night I would tie knots in a rope, wrap it about my waist, then try to sleep. St Rose had done this to mortify her flesh. I usually lasted about five minutes.

I knew I was weak.

When the new *Evening Press* was launched, Dad became 'The Night Reporter' and later wrote a daily column titled 'Dubliner's Diary'. He was supplied with a car, but he was a reckless driver.

If he was driving us to Dublin, he would check his watch as we set off, then tell us kids to keep an eye on the speedometer, while he attempted to 'break my record', by covering the sixteen miles in a minute or two less than the last journey. I thought it was very exciting – flying along at eighty miles per hour!

Not surprisingly, he had a couple of near misses. Once his car overturned into a ditch at Balrothery. He escaped unscathed. But a more serious crash, on an icy night near Dollymount, put an end to his driving days.

Walking home from school, I saw the *Evening Press* late news poster. 'Terry O'Sullivan injured in car accident.' I hurried home to find Mam huddled over a small fire in the playroom. 'It's not too bad. He broke some ribs and gashed his head.' She was quite calm.

But he took a long time to recover – lying on the sofa in the drawing room, unshaven, a deep cut on his temple, and uncharacteristically cross and grumpy.

He used taxis for his work after that – paid for by the *Evening Press* – but that didn't work out too well. Various acquaintances charged their taxis down to him. So, by the time 'Dubliner's Diary' became the social column to get a mention in, the *Press* had given him his own chauffeur-driven car, complete with a spotlight over his seat so he could write and read while being driven to his various engagements.

Rows between Mam and Dad were not uncommon. Mam had a terrific temper, which was made worse by Dad's controlled, modulated retorts. One night there was a tremendous racket going on in their long, hollow bedroom on the second floor. Dad locked Mam out on the landing, so she promptly fetched the hatchet and proceeded to bash open the door.

I was terrified up in my attic room, and ran down to Gráinne's room, which was all white and neat and tidy. We were instructed to knock before entry, but I burst in, forgetting to knock. She was awake of course – listening to the commotion. She pulled back her covers, and snuggled me in to her comfort.

'Pray with me Deirdre. We'll say the rosary.' Gráinne was very religious at the time. I fell asleep halfway through.

Next morning everything seemed quiet between Mam and Dad, apart from a few grazes and scrapes. They had made up. Nobody mentioned the splintered panel of their bedroom door.

It was never repaired either.

Mam collapsed one evening and was admitted to Our Lady of Lourdes Hospital in Drogheda.

Dad came home to us the first day. His eyes were red, he was unshaven and exhausted. 'Your mother is gravely ill. She's to have an operation. Pray for her.' His tone was grim. Mam had an operation to remove a gallstone and was anointed, but she pulled through.

About a week later, we were brought to see her. We were not allowed inside the hospital, so Mam waved out to us from the long, French windows of her private room. She looked beautiful – pale and thin in a soft, floaty nightgown. She seemed to glow with happiness too. Dad had been visiting her all the time, bringing flowers and presents and giving her lots of attention.

When she came back home and had recovered fully, her life and ours carried on in its normal muddle.

Sometimes when rain thundered down outside, I'd make a dash

for the giant willow tree with an old coat over my head. Squatting inside its base, I would listen to the mighty downpour lashing outside its circular branches which almost touched the ground. Only when huge drops penetrated its umbrella-like shape, and the dry carpet of browny twigs began to glisten with wet, would I run back into the house.

I went to see *Singin' in the Rain* in the local picture house, and was so entranced that I danced alone on the bare floor of my little room when I came home that night.

I had one friend. Her name was Phyllis Sharp. She lived with her uncle Jim in a tiny cottage. She had a round, rosy face, and jet-black hair with rigid waves. She was one year older than me and was beginning to show an interest in boys. When she got her period, I begged her to explain what it entailed. She said I'd have to wait for one whole year, and she promised on her word of honour, she'd enlighten me then.

I counted the months off, but I had left Balbriggan before the year was up.

SHADOWS

One balmy August afternoon, Terry, Don and I set off on a long country walk out Skerries way to look for bamboos. We pushed Noreen and Marian in a double buggy. They were two and three then, and were treated as twins, even though they were complete opposites. Noreen was skinny and long limbed with wisps of blond hair and saucer-like blue eyes. Marian was soft and smiling with a plump face and thick black hair. They loved each other and were very close.

As we bumped along the edge of the fields, a man approached and stopped our busy procession.

'Where are you off to?' He seemed pleasant enough.

We told him of our mission.

'I know where there's plenty of bamboo.' He pointed across a deep field. 'You couldn't bring the buggy, of course. If you come with me I can show you.'

He was looking only at me. A tiny doubt nudged, but the thought of the prized bamboo was tempting.

'All right. But Terry is coming with me. Don, you stay here with the girls, and we'll be back, real quick.'

I followed the man in through the tall, plush grass, with Terry trailing behind. The only sound was the crush of our shoes. Suddenly the man turned, knocked me flat, and jumped on top of me. His rough chin grazed my mouth.

'Terry, Terry!' I screamed. 'Run for help!' I struggled against his massive weight.

But Terry didn't run anywhere. I could see his skinny legs and corduroy trousers standing over us.

'Leave my sister alone!' He was shouting, feebly attempting to whack the man with a long stalk of a reed he'd been carrying. My nine-year-old brother.

But it worked.

The man clambered off me, and ran away through the long grass. I fixed my frock, and tried not to cry. I put my arm around Terry's slight shoulders.

'You're a great boy. I'm glad I brought you with me. Now promise you won't tell anyone about this, or I'll be in trouble.'

'All right.'

I could see this quiet little fella with the black cow's lick of hair falling over his forehead was all mixed up.

'Good boy.'

We ran back to the expectant faces of the little ones. Don wailed, 'Where's my bamboo? I want my bamboo. You promised.'

'There wasn't any in that field,' Terry answered for me.

I turned the buggy towards home. Noreen and Marian were starting to cry too. 'Now stop crying. We'll look for bamboo another time. Who'd like some honey-bee sweets? Mam gave me some money.'

They cheered up as we hurried along.

But I felt dirty. A cloud had crept across my innocence.

BOARDING OUT

'Please Daddy, let me go too.'

Nuala had been whisked off to boarding school amidst great excitement.

A shopping spree to Gorevan's of Thomas Street to buy her uniform – heavy grey wool coat and hat, sports outfits, her own personal counterpane, indoor shoes, outdoor shoes, tennis shoes, Sunday shoes and a dress. All this and her very own cutlery with the initials NOS engraved on each shiny utensil. Of course this caused endless problems at school, as our real name was O'Faolain. The store had used Dad's pen name – O'Sullivan.

Up in my attic room in Laragh House on the third floor, I hadn't even noticed, but apparently she had been sneaking out at night to liaise with undesirable fellows, so Dad decided boarding school was the best option for Nuala.

Gráinne had already left school, trained as a secretary, and had a good job in London.

I knew all about the wonders of boarding school. I'd read the English comics: Wasn't it all about first formers having wonderful adventures, tuck boxes and midnight feasts in the dorm?

Silly me.

At home, I was the 'good girl'. At twelve years old I was no trouble: quiet, shy, and very determined.

Dad gave in, and I too had my shopping outing. My cutlery was duly embossed DOS. My first ever name in print! Years after, rooting for a knife or a fork in the jumbled drawer at home, I could always pick out my very own.

Two weeks after the shopping trip, I stood alone in the courtyard of St Louis, Monaghan, surrounded by chattering girls greeting each other in fluent Irish. It had never occurred to me that this was an all-Irish school (I had only a few words), that Nuala had been sent there because of her rebelliousness, or that it had cost Mam and Dad huge money they could not afford.

I was terribly homesick, that first term. Within three weeks, I was thinking through Irish, but I missed my eccentric family, and dear, drab Balbriggan. I did make one friend, a tiny red-haired girl from Baltray, County Louth. Fidelma wore a long ponytail down past her bottom. Her flaming hair had not been cut since she was born.

She was lonely and lost like me.

BOARDING SCHOOL

The family had moved from Balbriggan to Clontarf while we were away at school, and we came home to a skinny, ugly, terraced house.

The night before I was due to begin *rang a dhó* in Monaghan, I waited up until very late in the front room. I heard Dad shut the front door and head up the stairs.

He stopped on the landing when I called him. I stayed down in the hall.

'Daddy, I've got to talk to you. I don't want to go back. Please don't make me…'

I stared up at him.

Only the year before I'd begged him to let me go.

***

I was miserable from the first day. Exiled. I hated nearly everything: the strict regime, the food, the loneliness. The only part I liked was the music. St Louis was well known for its choir, orchestra, operettas and plays.

Cold, dark, winter mornings. The six-thirty bell. The shiver of lino on warm feet. The rush to get dressed – everything perfect and exact. Tie knotted just so; cubicle tidied and shipshape; counterpane stretched taut; curtain pulled back – ready for inspection. And all in complete silence.

File down to Mass – such a long Mass – *as Gaeilge*. Then through the long corridors to the refectory for breakfast, stand behind the chair while grace is said, permission to talk at last. Porridge was the main food lumpy, grey stuff that I could never finish. But one morning a nun made me stay back after the others had left, and stood behind my chair until I had eaten the entire cold mess.

If a pupil wasn't well, she was allowed to stay on in bed until breakfast time. One night I pretended to have a cough. My cubicle was next to the nun's. I coughed and coughed loudly, until I fell asleep from exhaustion. Next morning I was given honey, lemon and glycerine, and allowed to wallow in my warm bed for a whole extra hour.

I tried the same trick again the following week, but it didn't work.

The Irish language was no problem; safe from outside influences, it became easier to absorb. But I struggled through the classes, except for English, which we learnt through Irish. Strange at first. We did *As You Like It*, my introduction to Shakespeare. I looked forward to that class.

I also started piano lessons. On the third floor, there were cupboard-like cubicles each with a piano, a narrow window and a private door. I loved practising my preliminary pieces up there, the afternoon sun shining through the window, the other girls out on the playing fields. Although I loved running, I was a coward when it came to games, except for basketball. Playing the piano wasn't dangerous like camogie, or embarrassing like tennis.

I rarely saw Nuala. She had lots of friends, was in a higher class than me, and her sleeping cubicle was miles down the dormitory. Academically she was very clever, doing all honours subjects through Irish.

I remember one night – the nun had been called downstairs –

we all squashed in behind Nuala's curtain to see her perform Johnny Ray's 'It Was a Night', a forbidden radio hit. Thrilled with fearful giggles at her boldness, we stood and watched as she gyrated from the waist upwards, squatting on her bed!

The *Mikado* was being staged while I was a pupil. I auditioned for a part, but was told my voice was too soft. Instead I was cast in a tableau as the young postulant, St Catherine Labouré. Dressed in a black dress and lacy veil, I had to pretend to be praying, then look up and gasp with delight at the apparition of Our Lady. She was in the centre of a huge medal which revolved around the stage.

Everyone said I would make a perfect nun after that. I considered it seriously for a week or so.

Food was a major issue, especially treats. Sweet things. For tea on Wednesday, there was always brown bread and jam. We would dash to the table in anticipation. On Friday, there was a sort of a shop, in a classroom, where pens and copies and a limited amount of Cadbury's chocolate bars were on sale. Unfortunately for me, sixth years were served first, then fifth, and so on down the line. By the time it came to *rang a haon*, if there was any chocolate left, I'd rarely have enough money to buy it after paying for my copy books.

Once Mam sent us a food parcel with a Gateaux cake in it. I hid it in my locker beside my bed and, after lights out, I would burrow my fingers into the box, grab a mushful, and cram it into my mouth. First thing next morning, I'd be sure to collect every minuscule crumb I'd spilled, so that there was no evidence.

On Sundays we donned our special Sunday dresses, coats and grey hats, and went for a long country walk, two by two. We were not allowed to stop or to talk to anyone. As we passed through Monaghan town, I yearned for the sweets, chocolate and comics I glimpsed as we marched past the forbidden shops.

At weekends our hair was inspected for head lice. The humiliation – seated on a chair in the narrow aisle between the sleeping cubicles. I was told to plait my hair and pin it on top of my head.

We had one job I loved: polishing the long, long strip of lino that ran the whole length of the dormitory. Thick pads were attached to our stockinged feet – after the polish had been rubbed in – then push, push, until the surface was smooth and shiny, and we could fly along in a free skid.

***

But now I stood, tense and hopeful, at the bottom of the stairs as I waited for Dad's answer.

'Of course I won't send you back if you feel that strongly. I'll have to make some phone calls in the morning. Now go to bed. And don't worry.'

I was so grateful. So happy. Free again. I slept like a log. Next morning, Dad woke me sharply.

'You're to get the bus to Eccles Street. Dominican Convent is the name of the school. Ask for the head nun. I've explained everything. Now, you'll need bus fare.'

His no-nonsense voice.

He dismissed my feeble thanks impatiently.

Later that morning I sat outside the office, waiting to see what class I was to attend. I was placed in second year, but within two weeks I was moved up to third year, as it became apparent that I had covered most of the course in St Louis. I began to realise what an excellent academic school it had been.

Nuala stayed on and sat her Leaving Cert through Irish and got first-class results.

***

The girls in my class were not very studious, and talked about boys most of the time. I decided I'd had enough of schools – six altogether – and that I should leave after my Inter Cert. Overall I hated school and having to stay put until the bell rang. I was timid and shy, not very noticeable, or popular, or brainy. I liked creative subjects, art and music, but in the rigid, conservative education system of the forties and fifties, they were bottom of the list.

Dad and Mam agreed with me. They had children attending different schools all over the place, and I had cost them a fortune!

Dad arranged for me to attend a commercial college in Fairview. I loved the clatter of the typewriters and the mysteries of Pitman's shorthand. No uniform to wear. Fifteen years old.

Out in the grown-up world at last.

We are going home for Christmas on the train!

At half five in the morning, twenty grey, uniformed young girls march two by two to the train station in complete silence. The frosty path crackles beneath our heavy black lace-up shoes, and the velvet sky shelters us above.

At last – freedom! The smell of the smoky train, the leather strap on the window of the curved door, the jerky start of the powerful engine, as we collapse in giggles on the faded plush seats. 'Cherry Pink and Apple Blossom White' is playing on the jukebox in Amiens Street Station. Forbidden English words tempting my ears for the first time in four months.

Deliciously dangerous sounds.

HARD FACTS

In the rented house in Clontarf, there was very little room or privacy.

When Nuala was at home, she and her teenage friends would gather around the fire in the dining room. Sometimes I was allowed to sit with them.

I glimpsed a new, exciting and dangerous world. They smoked cigarettes, wore tons of make-up, black figure-hugging sweaters with pointy breasts, tight straight black skirts, seamed nylons and high heels.

I thought they were gorgeous.

Her friend June was beautiful. Perfect heart-shaped faced, huge dark eyes, full lips, and long, wavy black hair. She was always kind to me. Sylvia was plumpish, with creamy white skin, long blond hair, and a husky voice. She smiled and laughed a lot. Vera sang Frank Sinatra's 'Learnin' the Blues' in a lazy, sophisticated drawl. Her hair was cut in a short bob and she had a super figure.

One night Sylvia decided that someone should tell me the facts of life. After some discussion, it was unanimously decided that it should be her.

She brought me into the front room and, much to my embarrassment, explained crudely that the woman just had to lie there while the man put his 'thing' inside her.

'It might hurt at first, but it gets better with practise,' she assured me. I quit the room as soon as I could.

I knew I would never be interested in that sort of carry-on!

As puberty beckoned, I became very self-conscious about how

I looked. One summer afternoon, I was wearing shorts and June told me I had lovely legs. I was so pleased.

I wore my first pair of seamed nylons on a trip to the shops with Nuala. Stepping behind me to observe my flesh-coloured legs, she commented dryly, 'You look ridiculous.'

I was crushed. Her opinion meant so much to me. She seemed so confident. So unafraid.

The only other person who commented on my appearance was Mam, who said constantly, 'Take that hair out of your eyes!' She always pointed out my 'Sullivan nose' when discussing family resemblances, so I had taken to draping a generous amount of my long hair casually over one eye and part of my nose.

In December 1955, during a lunch break from the Dominican Convent, I visited Mammy in the Rotunda Hospital. She had just given birth to my new brother, Dermot. Slight and tiny, he had huge eyes and a mop of black curls. Mam had her own penthouse suite, and was enjoying the luxury.

When she arrived home with the new baby, she looked marvellous in a new black two-piece Dad had bought her. But little Dermot's cot had to be put in the sitting room, and Mam declared the house was too small.

'I'm going to look for a bigger house, Tom, and this time we're going to buy. I'm sure you can afford it with your salary.

Not that I'd know what you earn!'

There was steely determination in her voice. Every house she had ever lived in had been rented. And now, with eight children and a mostly absent husband, there would be no stopping her.

'Right, Catherine. I'll leave it up to you. Let me know when you find something more suitable.'

And off went Dad in his chauffeur-driven Audi, smelling of aftershave.

Mam finally did it – bought their first home – and we all moved to Dollymount, to a big house with views of Dublin Bay.

Although there was lots of room, the house was old and in poor condition. Dad hired a decorator to paint the huge expanse of wall in the hall, stairs and landing. It was so large that an extra bed was put there for little Dermot. Rough sisal carpet was bought for the stairs. It attracted dirt, and proved to be uncleanable.

The nicest room in the house was the sitting room. A grand marble fireplace, square bay window, scarlet carpet on the stained wooden floorboards, and a second-hand chesterfield suite, covered with loose cotton covers. Small children were barred from this room except for special occasions. Folding doors opened up into the main family room: a bleak, lino-covered, dark place with an ugly, heavy table and a couple of uncomfortable chairs. There were gas fires in some of the bedrooms, but these were rarely lit. Coal fires in the dining room and the range down in the kitchen were our main source of heat. A lot of dirty work for Mam.

The days of having a maid were long gone.

I remember coming home from school one wintry afternoon, cold and hungry. There was no fire lighting. Mam was in a foul mood. 'If you want a fire, go out to the shed and fill a bucketful of coal,' she ordered. There was nobody else in the house. To my own surprise, I said 'No.' She glared at me. 'What did you say?' I started up the stairs.

'You heard me, I'm not your servant.' In a furious temper she raced up the stairs after me and, as I slammed my bedroom door in her face, she shouted over and over, 'How dare you! How dare you!'

I didn't see the misery her life had become. I was too immersed in my own exciting adolescence.

There was no routine, no shopping day; just up to the local shop when sugar or butter ran out. No fixed amount of money handed over to Mammy on a particular day. No financial arrangements between Dad and Mam. She usually asked him for money just before he set off for work. Anytime I was present, he affected an absent-minded, surprised tone. 'Of course, Catherine, how much do you need?' As though it had never entered his head. Yet final notices, ESB bills and telephone bills were stuck on a hook on a shelf in the kitchen. These were paid by priority, before the telephone was about to be cut off, or if legal proceedings were imminent.

Mam just muddled along in a haze of confusion. If money was needed for school or bus fare, it took some courage to ask for it, the usual answer being a distraught, 'Do you think I'm made of money? Ask your father.'

It wasn't that he was mean with money; he had always lived beyond his means, he just didn't seem to notice if a child needed shoes or a coat. He expected Mam to look after that sort of thing.

There was always heaps of washing to be done. Mam went through several washing machines; things got caught in the spinner, or the floor got flooded. A wooden airing line with a pulley was permanently groaning with the weight of clothes. It was positioned directly over the table, down in the dank flagstoned Victorian kitchen. Occasionally, during mealtimes, a soppy

59

trousers or frock would drop onto the table, only to be flung back up without a pause in the conversation.

The odd rat could be spied making its way around the ancient pipes where the kitchen wall met the ceiling. If I was having a cup of tea with friends, I would desperately chatter on so that their eyes wouldn't stray upwards!

Dad concentrated on the back garden. He bred precious roses, fed with the best fertiliser and, in summer, visitors were given a guided tour. He hid bottles of vintage wine in secret spots, and dug one up on special occasions with grand ceremony.

Every afternoon, dressed in his black evening suit, he'd head off to observe and partake in the social whirl of the Dublin scene. There he would be fêted and flattered so that a particular party might get a mention in his column, or a photo published. An unreal world, compared to the shambles back home.

Mam did try. On Saturdays she cooked us a dinner of mashed potatoes, sausages, gravy and onions, which we loved. We called it Snowball after a character in a radio serial we used to listen to. And on Christmas day, she slaved down in the kitchen, cooking the ham, turkey, spuds and vegetables, while Dad opened bottles of wine up in the dining room.

But mostly she escaped to the pub, leaving the chaos behind.

I had joined the Marian Arts Society in Mountjoy Square, where I met Anne, Carmel, and Nuala – three teenagers from the Malahide Road. We learned dancing and singing, and performed at shows to entertain the elderly. Every Thursday evening, my new friends would come out to Clontarf. We'd sit on my bed, painting our nails and discussing boys, the door firmly shut against the loneliness and neglect that was creeping through the rest of the household.

A LEAVE HOME

He left me home from the hop on the bar of his bike.

Dickie Rock and the Melochords were playing, and Eamon Brady had asked me up to dance three times. He was an apprentice bookbinder, earning twelve shillings per week – great money.

He was a terrific jiver. Wore smart suits and cream shoes. He had a thin face, and sleeked-back fair hair that never moved – held firm with lashings of Brylcream. But it was his soft, deep voice and long, tapered hands I secretly admired.

I fancied him shyly.
So did my best friend Carmel. We both thought Eamon Brady was gorgeous.

And now this desirable chap was gliding me home along the sparkly seafront of Clontarf.

I could feel the roughness of his heavy tweed coat graze against my face every time I turned my head slightly. His breath was in my hair – securely lacquered against the sea breeze.

I jumped down off the bike at our gate.

'Would you like to come to the matinee in the Fairview next Sunday afternoon?'

He was turning his bike around the way we'd come as he said it.

'I wouldn't mind. What's on?' I tried to sound casual.

'*Imitation of Life* with Lana Turner, I think. See you outside at three o'clock then?'

'All right. Goodnight. And thanks for leaving me home.'

He hopped onto his bike, then waved back at me with one hand as he pedalled off.

I stood and watched his dark, hunched figure shrink away along the deserted road. Then I twirled and skipped up the path.

'Wait till I tell Carmel!'

FACE TO FACE

I slipped out of my cuban-heeled shoes and gingerly opened the heavy front door.

As I tiptoed into the dark hall, a chink of light split the gloom, and Dad's head appeared from the bottom of the steps at kitchen level.

'I think you and I should have a little talk, Deirdre.' His voice was cold and calm.

He was still dressed in his evening suit. A handsome, middle-aged man, grey stubble on his firm jaw.

This stranger, my father.

I knew my place in his life. A vague, biddable, unobtrusive child.

'And how's daughter number three?' he'd enquire pleasantly, as we passed each other in the afternoon: he on his way out to his high-profile job, me coming home from commercial college.

Sometimes he left a note on the kitchen table – 'I'll leave you all my money' – when I laid out a treat after my cookery class on Tuesday nights. That had been his idea. I didn't mind at all. Actually, I liked it; it suited me. After all, I'd heard Mam say it enough times. 'Gráinne is the beauty of the family, Nuala the brainy one, and Deirdre the nice one.'

I was secretly pleased that he was worried about me coming home at two in the morning. Nobody in our sprawling, disorganised family ever noticed what I did, each wrapped up in their separate lives.

'Well?' His quiet, stony presence waited.

'I was at the pictures with a young man, Dad, and I missed the last bus from Fairview, so he walked me home.'

'Does this boy have a name?'

'His name is Eamon Brady. He lives on the North Strand. And he's not a boy. He's eighteen and a half. He works in Hely's of East Wall. It's a printing factory.'

I felt the sting of his hand on my face before I realised he had slapped me. I stood, shocked and still, as I watched him thump up the stairs, and heard the bedroom door slam.

***

Next day at commercial college, I typed furiously, trying to understand. Why had he lashed out at me? I had never witnessed him use physical tactics with us children. A curt epigram was enough of a rebuke. Certainly I had seen Dad with cuts and scratches on mornings following a fight with Mam. And she was spending more and more time up the road with her drinking buddies. He'd probably been drinking last night too.

He was rarely home in Clontarf. Gráinne was away in London, Nuala was living precariously in a bedsit in town somewhere, attending UCD, and there were five children younger than me needing schooling and love. Education was Dad's priority.

Noreen and Marian went to a Montessori pre-school and, when they were twelve and thirteen, they attended Sandymount High School. Terry was enrolled in Belgrove, then Belvedere College and finally Killester Technical School. Don kept mitching from school after school, ending up in Chanel College. All these had to be paid for.

The strain of being a charming, public man-about-town, an erratic husband and a mostly absent father was taking its toll.

***

That afternoon, I bought a tiny bunch of blue cornflowers from a snowy-haired old lady's flower stall. Silently I handed them to Dad as he emerged from the bathroom, freshly shaved. He bowed his head, and examined them intently as he chewed his bottom lip.

After a while he raised his eyes and looked at me.

'Thanks, chicken.' He patted my head.

I wished I could take away his hurt.

But the gulf was too vast.

WORKING INTERLUDE

Barely sixteen, earning my own money.

As soon as I started work, I went out to dances and pictures and got caught up in the excitement of Bull Wall trysts with my new pals.

I paid scant attention to what was going on at home in Clontarf.

I gave Mammy a few bob from my meagre wages every now and then, but sometimes when I got home in the evening there would be very little food in the kitchen. I would send one of the little ones up to the shop for a small sliced pan, and maybe a banana.

After making a snack for myself, I'd head upstairs and get dolled up – pale pink lipstick, mascara, newest item (maybe a scarf or nylons) and head off out.

My first job was in Ryan's Car Hire, Hawkins Street, beside the Theatre Royal. I was a clerk in the reservations department upstairs, typing out bookings – mostly for American tourists. Downstairs, in the front office, was the young team of managers, most of whom went on to glittering careers. Joe Malone, Dermot Ryan, Alan Glynn, Seamus Smith, and Bob Quinn.

I earned three pounds per week. After bus fares and lunches, I wasn't left with much. But such a thrill to be handed a brown envelope every Friday with my name on it!

Unlike the other girls, I was not a competent typist. I made mistakes repeatedly, and hid discarded letters in my handbag so that the wastepaper basket wouldn't look too full.

The novelty wore off pretty quickly, stuck in a pokey office all day, so I decided I'd head for London. At that time, Gráinne was working for the Irish Tourist Board there.

She sent me a strongly worded missive advising me against such a move. 'Too young,' she wrote.

So I moved to the O'Connell Street office of the *Evening Press* (Dad's name was a help).

I loved meeting the public, helping them compose ads, advising on wording, showing how money could be saved by paring down to the minimum. I got on well with the girls there. But when pressure was put on me to join the union, I decided to move again. I didn't like being tied down. I knew once I married I'd have to give up work – that was the law – so I wanted to sample as many different jobs as possible while I could. Anyway, my only ambition was to get married.

Over I went to Abbey Street – to MGM no less. They were preparing for the forthcoming premiere of *Ben Hur* in Ireland. For three months I addressed envelopes to invitees to this huge event. I felt very important.

Up to Suffolk Street next, to a dark, Dickensian office with latticed windows. Secretary to a middle-aged architect.

I typed out tenders for prospective customers. I made horrendous mistakes in the money columns and technical details of buildings. It took umpteen attempts to produce an accurate copy. Again the mistakes were stuffed in my handbag. Although ready to explode with tension, I'd casually place it on my boss's desk as if it had been no trouble.

I also worked the antiquated switchboard. But mostly I messed up. A customer would ring, I'd pull the connection out and plug in my boss's line. He'd tell me to 'put him through'. I'd forget which rope-like switch was which, plug in the wrong one, mix everything up, and cut off the client.

I dreaded the ring of the telephone.

For most of the week he travelled the country, so I just had to babysit the office, read my book, or take a stroll up Grafton Street when I was really bored. One afternoon I met his wife outside Switzer's, much to my embarrassment.

Time to move on.

Out to what was then considered to be the countryside to work for Gateaux Ltd in Finglas. I held the important position of secretary to Mr Hohn. We shared a swanky office. He was from Switzerland, and had introduced the Swiss roll to Ireland. Mr Hohn was getting on in years and his son had taken over most of his duties, so we didn't have much to do. He seemed to enjoy my company, and chatted about cakes and his home country. Sometimes I made reservations for him over the phone to Lake Lucerne, in my rusty school French.

I had such a long journey from Clontarf that I was always late. But he didn't seem to mind.

I helped count the wages for the factory staff every Friday, but maths was not my forte.

There was often great delight when a confectioner got an extra 'raise' in his pay packet, or consternation when a shortage was discovered.

I was asked to organise the holiday roster instead.

That went slightly awry. I had a huge crisscross list of

fortnights. The senior staff members chose their slots first, and I wrote their names opposite their choices. Somehow I put down too many people for the first two weeks in August, and there were lots of arguments when the list was posted!

But I must have done something right, because when I left – to get married – they gave me a wedding cake and, the latest thing, a transistor radio. The little radio was my pal for years.

I am just nineteen and Mam is pregnant again. Overweight and miserable, with swollen ankles.

She sits in the sitting room with her legs propped up on a stool as my girlfriends and I jive to the latest rock'n'roll record in front of her. I am wearing a puffed-out skirt, tightly nipped in at the waist with a black 'waspy' belt. Acutely aware of my youth and vigour, I bop like mad.

'You're all marvellous dancers. Such lovely figures…' she calls after us, as we hurry out the door to our weekly hop.

PULLING AWAY

I was going steady with Eamon and socialising with his family. I witnessed their orderly family life and that of my friends and decided that this was the kind of world I wanted. I was leaving the remnants of my family to fend for themselves.

Mam's ninth child was born in 1960. Baby Niamh was tiny and undemanding. She slept in a cot in Mam and Dad's room. Nights they didn't hear her cry, I would lift her out and feed her Cow & Gate formula.

Everyone doted on her, and whoever was at home looked after her.

One Saturday in December, I came home from town to find Mam and Dad down in the kitchen.

'I got engaged today, and we put a deposit on a new house,' I announced shyly.

Mam was first to speak.

'To that young chap Eamon? That's nice dear. And where is the house?'

'It's not built yet. It's in Artane.'

'But that's miles away!'

Dad took over – businesslike.

'And when might you be getting married?'

'Thirtieth of July next.'

'Well, remind me to pay for Gráinne's wedding first, will you? Now I must dash…car's waiting…well done!'

BRADYS

When Eamon and I began to go steady, his family tucked me into their lives, and I almost became one of them. They lived noisily and happily, all squashed together in a small, terraced house off the North Strand.

Mrs Brady's father, Joseph Byrne, a tall handsome man, originally from County Kildare, had bought the first five houses in the street so that he could amalgamate the back gardens into one long yard. He then divided it into sheds, and raised cows right there.

He lived in the first house, with a shop out front, and a milk dairy at the rear. He gave a house each to some of his children, and the cost of a house – a few hundred pounds then, to the others.

In 1954, when the bridge over the Tolka River collapsed in the cold December dark, North Strand and Fairview were flooded. Some of Mr Byrne's cows drowned, trapped in their feeding pens. He managed to save some of them, racing against time, plunging under the icy black water to release their locks.

Downstairs in the Bradys' house was underwater, so the family had to stay upstairs. Soldiers distributed rough, grey, army blankets from rowboats. From the bedroom door, Eamon could see a sideboard and his violin case floating below in the mucky darkness.

When I met up with the Brady bunch, Eamon's granny Byrne and his aunty Tish ran the shop and dairy. On the landing of their house was a door which led into the next house.

That's where the Bradys lived.

Eamon told me that when he was a little boy he was often sent on errands through this shortcut.

'The landing was dark and gloomy. There was a stuffed dog in a glass case in front of the tiny window, and I had to pass it to open the door. It terrified me. I would stamp my feet up our stairs as fast as I could, then race down my granny's stairs.'

Mrs Brady was a neat lady, with lovely dark eyes behind small circular spectacles, high cheekbones, and a wide thin mouth. When she was going somewhere, she powdered her whole face, liberally applied dark red lipstick, then immediately wiped it all off with a handkerchief. She put rigid waves in her fine hair by heating an old hair tongs on the gas ring. She would test it first on a piece of paper. If it didn't go on fire, the tongs was applied to her hair. Her hair was regularly singed.

She cooked, cleaned, ironed, and waited hand and foot on her family of eight children.

Always at home to callers, she loved a chat in front of the huge fire, which she cleaned out and lit every morning for ten months of each year.

On Saturday nights she bathed the small children in a huge tin bath – filled with kettles from the stove – then polished all their shoes and laid out their clean Sunday clothes. When most of them had been packed off to bed, she would open her weekly treat – a bottle of Winter's Tale sherry – and make the stuffing for the chickens.

Mrs Brady always had a cigarette pursed between her lips when she was working. Whether peeling potatoes, cooking, or washing dishes. The ash invariably dropped off into the sudsy water, or potato sack, as she had no free hands to extract it from her mouth.

The front door of Mrs Brady's house opened onto the street footpath. Her house, and it was her house – Mr Brady said he 'just hung up my hat' – consisted of a parlour, which was only used on special occasions, and a narrow hall leading down to the main dining-room-cum-kitchen-cum-bathroom. Face and teeth were washed at the kitchen sink, and permanent mountains of washing hung in multiple lines under the steamy glass-roofed kitchen. Two bedrooms upstairs and an outside toilet. No garden, no yard.

Yet Mrs Brady managed to grow daffodils and even a rose bush, by piling earth onto a lean-to between the back door and the loo.

She was generous to a fault. Vast dinners were cooked every day for one o'clock. The same menu each week.

Eight pork chops on Monday. Tuesday and Saturday were stew days – bottomless stews with barley, kidneys, and steak. Anyone who dropped in was sure of a bowl. Wednesday was corn beef and cabbage day; Thursday, steak and onions or sheep's hearts; and Friday was smoked cod in a white onion sauce. Occasionally, tripe would appear – a favourite of Eamon's.

All this food, plus cigs, treats for the children, and one bottle of sherry would be written down in the well-thumbed accounts book of the local shop, to be settled each Saturday. Mrs Brady never managed to clear it completely.

Mr Brady was very careful with money, and hated any sort of waste. He had given up smoking as a young man, and nagged at Mrs Brady.

'You don't even inhale, Rita!' he'd remind her, in an exasperated tone, or, as she peeled thick skins into the sack of potatoes, 'You're throwing half the potatoes away.'

He bought her a potato peeler as a present.

Eddie Brady was a self-made man, and a hard worker. He ran a vegetable round, raised pigs, and later chickens, over in his 'yard' in Spring Garden Street. Everyone knew him as the 'vegetable man'. He wasted nothing; scraps, peels and leftovers, were collected for his pigs and chickens. He always kept a bucket of mush in his old red van. The odour mingled with the apple and vegetable smell.

He was a small, solid man with a florid complexion and heavy black glasses that slipped halfway down his pointed nose. On his rounds he wore the same brown felt hat and coat, shiny with age, and a leather money satchel crossed over his shoulder. This contained his account book, detailing every penny he was owed, and the names of his debtors.

Each evening after his tea, he washed himself by the kitchen sink, put on his good overcoat, and went up to his local for his few pints. Mrs Brady didn't mind at all. She helped the children with their homework on weekdays. Her little luxury was to go up to bed early with her book. When she was reading *Lady Chatterley's Lover* she could be heard from downstairs, laughing loudly at the naughty bits.

On Saturday, when Mr Brady gave Rita her 'wages', he would firstly deduct the amount she owed for vegetables, eggs and potatoes! He was wary of Rita's generosity. To her money was for spending, though rarely on herself. He saved every penny he could.

Yet the children never wanted for anything. I was amazed at the presents they had acquired over the years. A real billiard table with ivory balls, a huge, tin rocking horse, Meccano sets, a radiogram in polished wood. And he was the first on the street to buy a television set.

He sent the older children to music lessons. Angela, the eldest, learned to play the piano, and Eamon and Joseph learned the violin. Eamon and his mother were musical, but the others weren't. When Joseph was sent up to the parlour to 'practise', he would open the case, and drag the bow across the strings, without bothering to take the violin out.

Nobody noticed the difference.

There was a battered out-of-tune piano in the parlour where Mrs Brady would plonk out old songs at party time. Mr Brady could be very entertaining when he was 'merry'. He often sang a rather risqué song, 'A German Clockmaker'.

When Granny Byrne decided that she was dying, she took to her bed. Mrs Brady looked after her, running up and down the stairs through the door on the landing. I went in to visit the old lady in her fine, large bedroom. A Chinese screen hid a claw-footed bath over by the window. The water was heated by some contraption piped up through the floorboards. This is where the adults from both families took a bath on special occasions – mostly on the eve of weddings.

There was a wooden trunk at the foot of the vast mahogany bed. Granny Byrne instructed me to open it and take out her white starched habit – for her laying out. The poor lady was all ready to meet her maker, but he was in no hurry to receive her.

Mr Brady bought a ramshackle wooden structure overlooking

the sea in Rush, County Dublin. Every year, Mrs Brady, the children, pots, pans, and chattels were all packed into his red van and deposited there for the whole summer.

Apart from the main door, curtains on a plastic line covered the entrance to the two main bedrooms. One for the men, and one for all the Brady ladies – young and old. In the girls' room, two double mattresses were pushed together, so that making the beds meant crawling across them and dragging the covers up.

The first time I visited Rush to stay overnight, a future mother-in-law of Eamon's brother, Joseph, was staying also. I had to sleep right next to her – crushed up against the wooden partition that separated us from the boys' room. We were complete strangers. I don't know which of us was the most embarrassed!

There was a chemical toilet outside for all the gang. Early each morning, before anyone was awake, Mrs Brady dug a deep sandy hole, then buried the contents of 'Elsie'.

Mr Brady came to stay at weekends, and brought Mrs Brady out to the pub on Sunday.

He wasn't exactly speedy with the rounds, and sometimes when he'd say, 'What are you having, Rita?' she'd ask for ten cigarettes instead of a drink – much to his annoyance.

Mr Brady was very strong, and very stubborn. Never sick. He owned an old house in Fairview which he let out as flats. One afternoon, when he was clipping the hedge there, he impaled himself on the railings. The pointed iron went up under his ribs. He resolutely pulled his body free, but refused to have hospital treatment.

In his late sixties, as the ravages of cancer crept through his body, he ignored it for as long as he could, dragging himself to work, and even up to the pub, though he could barely stomach a drink.

In his final weeks, Mrs Brady nursed him at home. He was a difficult patient, refusing to give in or let go. He would only take painkillers near the very end. 'Am I banjaxed, Rita?' he burst out one evening. But he didn't really want to know the answer.

His last day was a Saturday. All his family, and myself, stood in the shaded bedroom, our eyes never straying from his wracked face. The only sound his rasping breath, labouring in and out, in and out.

Then strangely there was nothing. His chest didn't rise anymore. He was still. It was so simple. I had never witnessed anyone dying before. It was hard to comprehend. Here was this man who had talked, worked, laughed, sung, for well over sixty years and now, by just stopping breathing, he was gone.

I left the family, and walked up to the butchers on the North Strand to collect Mrs Brady's ham for Sunday.

After Mr Brady's death, wads of musty notes rolled up in elastic bands were found under his bed. Mrs Brady shared it out amongst her eight children. Later on, the bank informed her that she was now the owner of quite a nice amount of money, so she booked a trip to Lourdes for herself. She had wanted to go all her life. At sixty-seven years of age, she was to fly in a plane for the first time. We all saw her off at Dublin Airport. We joined the queue for those checking in, and every time it moved a little, Rita – and about twenty of us – shuffled forward.

With her short-lived wealth, Mrs Brady also booked one week's holiday in Mosney Holiday Camp for all her children, daughters-in-law and grandchildren. They had a row of chalets beside each other and it cost over two thousand pounds. We didn't take up her kind offer – we stayed in the chalet in Rush, but Mrs Brady bought us expensive presents in Mosney instead.

There was great surprise and consternation when she announced that she was going to work in Boyer's of North Earl Street. Rita had never had a job outside of her family in her whole life. Before she was married she had delivered milk in billycans from the dairy.

The older children said they would give her some money each week, but she would not budge.

She told me she liked getting out of the house for a change, and enjoyed her job as a cleaner. She polished the brass doors and stair banisters, and chatted with the staff and customers. Her employee account was always in the red at Christmas. She had a knack for suiting the right present to the person. I got my first ever expensive French perfume for my birthday, and everyone had samples or bargains she had brought home. She got Mass in the Pro-Cathedral most days after work and, every Saturday, seven large chickens were ordered from Geraghty's of Marlborough Street. One for each of Mrs Brady's married offspring, along with one pound of the best quality sausages.

Mrs Brady rarely visited anyone. Everybody came to her home; an invitation was not needed, there was always a welcome. Neighbours, children, babies, in-laws, just pushed open the heavy front door, called down the hall, and walked on in.

NEW YEAR

New Year's Eve, 1961.

Such a wonderful, exciting time. Best ever. To be nineteen, healthy, alive and glowing.

And to be in love.

Eamon and I had just become engaged. We hadn't a care in the world. We were celebrating with his family at their home. The boisterous Brady bunch.

It was snowing all over the city – the icing on this magical night. We threw snowballs at each other out on the muffled pathways, laughing in each other's arms. Young, handsome, and free.

I knew I looked gorgeous in my new clothes – tight black wool dress, two-inch-high purple pointed shoes, and a new navy duffel coat. I had paid ten shillings off it each week for twelve long weeks – a huge sum from the three pounds per week wages I earned as a secretary in Gateaux Ltd. I had collected it that very day from Cassidy's of North Great George's Street.

I was so happy – snowflakes in my shiny black hair. My ring, a blue aquamarine stone encased by four little diamonds, twinkled up at me by the light of the streetlamps.

'Quick. It's starting in a few minutes.' Mrs Brady poked her head out the front door. In we dashed, down the narrow hallway, squashing through the crowd in the kitchen until we claimed a space.

We all waited. In silence.

Then we saw it for the first time – the St Brigid's cross, with

79

'Telefís Éireann' in big white letters beneath it. Our own Irish station at last. We cheered – elated and proud. We watched the fuzzy pictures relayed from the Gresham Hotel, the jovial crowds, the snow. So strange – barely one mile away from O'Connell Street.

Eamon's granny Byrne – a spry, bony old lady with a fuzz of white hair, dipped her hand into the pocket of the blue nylon housecoat she always wore over her good clothes, and took out a bashed cigarette. She always smoked one on very special occasions.

At midnight, the light was switched off, but the television flickered at us, the volume turned up full blast, as we hugged and kissed each other in the half dark.

'Happy New Year!'

A chorus of voices cheered.

I wanted to hold on to this night for always.

But I sensed that somehow, that heavy square newcomer on the sideboard, innocently relaying its grey-white shadowy images, had made an uneasy difference. It was the beginning and the end.

MAUREEN

My aunty Maureen burst upon the drab, mundane world of Dublin in the 1950s when she arrived home from the West Indies with Eoin, her husband, and two beautiful children.

Fluffy-haired, blue-eyed Eileen and baby Margot, christened Margosita, black-haired and dark-eyed. They moved in with Granda, or 'Pop' as Maureen always called him, to 122 Clonliffe Road.

About ten years younger than my mother, who was her eldest sister, Maureen was in her late twenties then. Vivacious and unconventional, she was skinny and tall, with long arms and legs. She had a tan from years of living in the tropics, even, white teeth – Eoin had treated her to crowns for a birthday present – and crinkly green eyes. Her shoulder-length, wavy red hair, a burnished copper, was usually tied up in a gay bandana or constantly combed back through her fingers when it was loose and shiny.

She was always singing around the house, native rhythms like 'Brown-skinned Girl', or Spanish tunes like 'Perfidia'; or 'I, yi, yi, yi, Quante Le Ore'. She laughed a lot too – threw back her head and laughed until the tears squeezed from her eyes.

I thought she was wonderful.

At first, toddler Margot, who had been born in Caracas, Venezuela, was an extension to Maureen's hip, clinging to her safety, as she did not understand English. I loved the soothing foreign words and songs between mother and child. I remember one word – *basta* – uttered frequently when Margot got into a tantrum.

81

Maureen and Eoin had married in Trinidad in the sunshine. He had been working with Maureen's brothers in their deep-sea diving business. He was a tall, strong, fair-haired, gentle man from Tralee, County Kerry. He had a soft lilting accent, and was a lovely singer. His song was 'When April Showers Come Your Way'.

Now Eoin wanted to buy a fishing trawler with his savings, so he invested the lot in an old boat moored in Howth Harbour.

Recklessly, Maureen ordered new furniture for Granda's dull, dark house. The folding doors between Granda's bare, back room and the front room were opened up permanently. It was transformed into a proper dining room, with a white tablecloth and real linen serviettes in holders. A three-piece suite was installed in the sitting room and new net curtains brightened up the long, slim windows.

When I was attending the Dominican Convent, I would walk down to 122 for my dinner, which always included dessert. My spirits would lighten in anticipation whenever I'd spy a favourite of mine on the sideboard. Jam Swiss roll, soaked in fruit juice, smothered in creamy custard.

Maureen didn't eat anything herself, but served Granda, the little girls and me first, while a mug of tea sufficed for her. She would sit, chin resting on her cigarette-holding hand, her mouth curled with laughter, as she regaled us with tales about her life in the West Indies.

In Trinidad they had lived in a large bungalow with a cool veranda, overlooking the sea. They had black servants and nanas for the children. Maureen read, swam, entertained, and led a glamorous life. She drank a lot too.

If a hot day chanced upon Granda's bleak back yard, she would drop everything, don her shorts, bring out a cushion, her cigs and book, and perch, knees bent, hunched up against the grey walls of the narrow, concrete yard.

Maureen bought hanging baskets, filled with scarlet geraniums, and hung them on the walls outside the kitchen and scullery windows.

She had her ungainly monster of a washing machine shipped to Dublin, and there was great fuss and curiosity from the neighbours the day it was delivered. It was the first electric washing machine I had ever seen. A large circular tub, squat on two legs with wheels, washed the dirty clothes. A roundy spinner attached to it stood on one leg. When in use, it waltzed around the scullery, the two lids banging and clanging, while we shouted above the racket.

Maureen taught me the rudiments of domestic life. How to set a table, how to iron, how to fold a shirt properly. She brought me upstairs and showed me the way to sort clothes; separate drawers for undies, socks. She explained basic hygiene; the correct way to brush my teeth, groom my hair, change underwear every day. Simple things I hadn't known.

I was walking down Clonliffe Road one school day on my way to lunch, when I got my first period. I was fourteen and a half. I was thrilled and scared. All topsy turvy. Delighted, because I had been worried I would never be the same as my friends who'd had their periods for years already, and afraid because I didn't know much about the process.

Maureen explained everything to me simply and naturally. She gave me money and a note and sent me down to the corner shop.

Red-faced, I gave it to the lady behind the counter. She scanned it discreetly, then handed me a bulky brown paper bag.

That afternoon, when I got home to Clontarf, Mammy was under the stairs putting shillings in the gas meter.

I addressed her bent-over back. 'Maureen told me to tell you I got my period today.'

'That's good dear,' she murmured absently.

I heard the hollow click of the coins as they dropped into the meter.

***

When I finished school to attend commercial college, I continued to visit 122, daily, and often babysat. Maureen now had little baby Mary, born in Dublin.

By the time Eamon and I had started to go steady, he was welcome there too.

Sometimes I would break it off, when the crush of two opposite lifestyles overwhelmed me. The rigid pattern of the Bradys, everything mapped out neatly – home, school, job, and finally marriage. The bohemian existence of my family in Clontarf; no routine, no firm plans, no set time for meals, no bath night. Mammy and the younger children co-existing under the same roof, yet each in their own private world.

Eamon would call on his lunch break to try and patch things up between us. Maureen would usher him in to the sitting room, then shoosh me up the stairs from the kitchen to 'talk to that nice fella'. She had no hang-ups about class or gender, unlike Daddy. He had asked me, 'What does this young man's father do?' and was distinctly unimpressed when I replied boldly, 'Mr Brady is a vegetable man.'

It took Dad a while to accept Eamon, who in turn was very shy on the rare occasions they met. Mam barely noticed what I was doing, but was always vaguely amicable towards Eamon.

Back home from our honeymoon, we moved into a bedsit in Summer Street, not far from Clonliffe Road. It consisted of one huge room, plus a bedroom over an arched laneway. We prettied it up, curtaining off the kitchen area, and hung a mirror on the drab walls. It cost extra to have a bath, and the landlady had to be notified so that the gas geyser was turned on.

I was alone all day while Eamon was at work. I knew nobody, and had nothing to do. I used to walk slowly along Ballybough Road and spend ages choosing a tea-strainer or colander, as we were fairly poor.

On Fridays I packed our dirty laundry into our honeymoon case and got the bus out to Clontarf to do our weekly wash. Most other days I would walk to 122, and help Granda and Maureen with the kiddies. Maureen was expecting another baby, skinny as ever, with a firm bump in front.

Eoin's fishing-boat business was not working out. The engine clapped out, then bad weather and red tape combined to force him to give it up. All his savings were gone.

So he went over to London to work. The family were to join him when he was up and running and could buy a house.

Maureen was not one for staying in nights. She socialised about town, even when she was pregnant, and we minded the children.

Baby Eugene was born in the Coombe Hospital. Eamon and I went to see him. Maureen asked Eamon to nip out to the pub on the corner to buy her a baby Power. When he brought it back, she hid it under her pillow.

As soon as she was back home in 122, her drinking started to take over. The pristine house she had run effortlessly began to fall apart. She rarely ate and smoked non-stop. Borrowed money. She 'sold' us her washing machine for two pounds. The mink coat Eoin had bought her disappeared to the pawnshop.

Granda tried to halt the decline. 'For the love of Mike, woman!' he'd declare in exasperation when she asked him for money for cigarettes or 'essentials'. They both knew what it was for. Empties were hidden in the scullery, the coal shed, the hallstand.

Her health deteriorated.

Strangely enough, she seemed happy. She adored her four beautiful children, showered them with love and hugs, sang to them, told them stories. It was new to me to see spontaneous signs of affection. At home we never went in for hugs and kisses. A pat on the head was the nearest Dad ever ventured. Mammy might grab hold of my hand when she was sad and drunk. That was about it.

One day I came across a pool of blood on the kitchen floor in 122. Maureen was upstairs in bed, propped up with a pillow, a book balanced on her knees.

'What's wrong Maureen? Will I get the doctor for you?'

'I'm fine, Di. It's just female trouble. I'm getting up in a while. Don't worry. Now be a dear and nip across the road for a baby Power. It helps the cramps. You needn't say anything to Pop.'

I tried to persuade her to get Lucozade instead, but she just laughed at my serious face.

Maureen's older brother Terry, or Uncle Buddy as we knew

him, came over from London with his wife Peggy and had a talk with Eamon and me. They had arranged treatment for Maureen in England, and asked us to move into 122 to look after the children with Granda, who had written to them about her condition. Of course we said yes. We loved the kiddies and got along fine with Granda. There was plenty of room in the four-bedroomed house, so we moved in.

Six weeks later, Maureen returned, thinner and quieter, but in good form.

'I haven't touched a drink for months!' she promised Granda gaily. She told her delighted children that their daddy had bought a house for them all in London, and they were to travel over on a huge ship to join them.

Dad sent two Princess cars to collect Maureen, her children, Eamon, Mammy and me. He and Maureen had socialised a lot together, without Mammy.

Granda stood at the edge of the porch – on his head the squashed peaked cap he always wore, his hands thrust deep into his pockets. He leaned forward slightly to nod goodbye as the cars pulled away.

The little ones were bursting with excitement as we all clambered aboard the ship.

'Di and Eamon, will you show the children their cabin? Catherine and I won't be long.' Maureen turned in the opposite direction. We played on the bunks until the hooter sounded. I went to look for Maureen and Mam. I saw them through the glass doors of the bar, sitting up on high stools at the counter.

Enjoying their drink.

Eamon and I stayed on with Granda. The house reverted back to dull quietness. On my twenty-first birthday I knew for sure I was pregnant. Our baby was due in late October.

By the following September, Maureen was gravely ill in hospital in London. Cancer of the bowel. Granda went over to see her – he was over eighty at the time, and when he returned he told us that somebody would have to mind her children while Eoin was at work. He suggested that I go – the kiddies knew me. But I was too afraid. What if our baby came early?

Mammy surprised us all by taking the initiative and declared she would travel instead. She looked after the little ones and visited the hospital in the evenings.

Maureen knew that she was dying. 'I don't mind for myself, but I hate leaving the children,' she had told Granda.

She died on 1 October 1963. She was thirty-four years old. Reckless, charming, unpredictable. I loved her unquestionably.

I could have gone to London after all. Ciarán, our son, didn't arrive until four weeks later.

LEAVING

On the morning of my wedding, I got up at seven o'clock to have my breakfast, as I had to fast for Holy Communion. Everyone else was sleeping. I was getting married at eleven o'clock. I went back to bed, and set my alarm for ten. I called all the family – nobody got up.

I sat on my bed looking out at the sea.

Then I darned a hole in the veil my friend had given me. I took out my rollers, brushed my hair, put on the plain dress I'd had made, new white shoes, then painted my nails.

I called everyone again. It was like an ordinary morning. I helped my two little sisters get dressed, then Dad called and said the car was outside.

After the church and photos we drove to the reception. We'd been there eight months earlier for my sister's wedding. The meal wasn't a success. The seating arrangement had mixed up strangers with strangers, so it was quite a stilted, formal affair.

But once the music started I let my hair down, and danced all afternoon to Cliff Richards and Bill Haley. I drank Babychams and felt beautiful.

Too soon I had to change into my 'going away' outfit – grey suit, velvet hat, and blue bag, gloves, and shoes.

As I stood in the guest bedroom in my white satin slip, Eamon opened the door.

'Will you be long? We have to get to the ship by half eight.'

I grabbed my jacket and held it across my chest.

'Get out! Can't you see I'm not properly dressed,' I shouted at his amazed face.

He shut the door quickly and left me alone.

Then it dawned on me. He was my husband now. We were really married.

I had expected to feel differently. I thought I was a sensible young lady – doing everything by the book – a mature twenty-year-old. But just then I realised; I knew nothing. The future was unknowable. The only certainty was that I was Mrs Brady now, and there was no going back.

I was scared.

FUNNYMOON

When Eamon and I got married, our family and friends thought we were brave young people to travel as far as Spain!

Neither of us had ever been outside of Ireland before.

We arranged everything ourselves by post. We chose San Sebastian from a black-and-white brochure. It was to be a ten-day adventure over land and sea. There were no direct flights or package holidays in 1962.

Eamon got a precious fourteen days off from the printing factory. I, of course, had left my employment (married women were not allowed work outside the home!). Eamon would support me.

We got married on Monday, as my father-in-law wouldn't take Saturday off because it was his busiest day. After the reception, Dad accompanied us out to Dún Laoghaire. He boarded the ferry with us.

'I've a surprise for you two!' he chuckled, as he led us up to the top deck. He knocked on the door of a large 'Private' cabin. A charming man stepped out – all smiles.

'This is the First Engineer. A good friend of mine. He is kindly loaning you his own cabin for your night's crossing.' Dad beamed.

I glimpsed a warm, cosy, carpeted room. A large four-poster bed. Latticed window over a desk laden with books and a radio. It was magic. Just like the ones I'd seen in films.

My brand-new husband's shaky voice interrupted my effusive thanks.

'There's no need, Mr O.' Thanks all the same. Deirdre and I

have booked our own cabin,' he declared proudly.

With embarrassed apologies all round, we said goodbye, and went to look for our 'cabin', as the ship pulled out.

We found it all right – deep in the bowels of the boat. A third-class cupboard. No porthole, just two skinny bunk beds. It was so narrow, Eamon had to step outside while I undressed. Then I climbed up to the top bunk so that he could come back in!

So our wedding night passed on the heaving, bockety, stuffy ship. Me in my pink 'baby-doll' nylon nightdress. No romance.

At seven o'clock the next morning, we gate-crashed first class for breakfast. Blearily, I watched, fascinated, as the salt and pepper slid from one end of the table to the other, in tune with the rolling boat.

That afternoon we arrived in Euston Station. A jumble of grey-faced, pinstriped, bowler-hatted city gents. We ate plastic-tasting sandwiches on a bench, then set off, on foot, carrying our huge brown leather suitcases – to look for Maida Vale.

I had picked this address out of an Irish newspaper. It sounded posh, so I booked a B&B there.

'We'll stay in an expensive place for our first night,' I had suggested.

When we found it – a crumbly, rundown house – a cranky woman read us out a list of do's and don't's. We asked for sandwiches. Not a chance. We ate a bar of chocolate instead, washed up in the bathroom down the hall, said our prayers, then climbed into the double iron bed.

Our religion was very important to Eamon and me, and we had attended devotions to Our Lady of the Miraculous Medal every

Monday night during our engagement – to help with self-control and to keep us pure. So we were both virgins on our wedding day.

Nobody talked about sex then – neither family, friends, nor even ourselves.

So now here we were – married – together in a big bed, but we were not too sure what went where! After a while we gave up, exhausted, and fell into a badly needed sleep.

We had asked the landlady to call us at seven o'clock – we had to get to Victoria Station to catch our coach to San Sebastian. She didn't. Breakfastless, we had to over-tip a taximan to make it on time.

We were the only young Irish honeymooners on the coach. The other passengers were mostly retired British couples.

Wednesday morning we left London for Dover. Despite a cold, windy ferry to Ostend, a shattered windscreen near Lille, a border check at Biarritz – where we were asked to step off the bus and our new green passports were scrutinised – we arrived in San Sebastian at noon on Thursday. A dignified, grand old city, curving around the bay.

Cramped and sleepless, Eamon and I dumped our cases at the villa where we were to stay with the other occupants of the coach. Starved for fresh air and privacy, we changed into our new swimwear and headed for the deserted beach. It was really hot, but the sky was overcast. We stretched out on the roasting sand and fell asleep.

Three hours later we awoke, badly sunburned. We had covered our bodies in Ambre Solaire oil (no mention of SPF then!). No one had told us about siestas in August. That night we slept separately – barely able to tolerate a sheet next to our raw skin.

During our brief few days there, we seemed to be the only Irish people in all of San Sebastian. True foreigners. Spanish folk used to stare in curiosity at our Sweet Afton cigarette packets.

We were just about recovered from tiredness and sunburn when it was time for our four-day return journey home.

The 'cheaper' B&B we had booked for our overnight on the way back was just that.

The door to our bedroom didn't open fully, as a single bed was practically up against it, the other single butted to the wall. We made sure to get a British breakfast next morning, and dressed in the trendy outfits my brother Terry had bought abroad and given us for our wedding present. He had been travelling the world with Irish Shipping.

'To go to sea, you had to be a member of the Seaman's Union, but you could not get a card unless you had been to sea already.' Mammy knew a man who knew somebody, so off Terry had sailed on the *Irish Sycamore* as a deck hand. 'I worked my way up to EDH – experienced deck hand,' he informed me proudly.

I had to open my case on the train to Liverpool and change out of my lovely new pale blue cotton pedal pushers into a crumpled skirt, as my period arrived unexpectedly.

Arriving in Holyhead, our spirits dropped when we saw that we were to sail home on the *Princess Maud*. It was infamous because it had no stabilisers. We had no cabin booked and spent the night stepping over heaving bodies and pools of vomit, trying to find a tiny space to sit on our hard, wobbly suitcases.

Drained, peeling, broke and bedraggled, in the grey dawn

light, we at last stepped back thankfully onto Irish concrete. I felt as though we had been away for months. Spain seemed a million miles behind us.

I felt as though everyone in Dublin should gasp with delight when they saw us – line the streets, clap, shout, 'welcome home, well done. You made it!'

Nobody gave us a second glance as we trudged through the morning drizzle to catch the bus for Clontarf. Home to Mam.

She was still in bed – reading her book. She peered over her glasses at my wan young face.

'You don't look married, dear. You haven't got stars in your eyes,' she murmured accusingly.

JUST US TWO

Eamon had only left for work on his Motobi scooter when I felt the first contraction. Wow! This was going to be the day: 6 November 1963.

I snuggled back into our still-warm bed and took out my maternity book. It said I had thirty minutes before the next contraction.

My mind was a jumble of thoughts.

Now Deirdre, keep calm…plenty of time…sort everything out in your head…butterflies of delight…we'll have our first baby by evening surely…have to leave our cosy bedsit, no babies allowed… But the pains…will I be able to bear them? Fear. And Eamon…we would never be just us two again…sadness…would I be a good mother? Was I too young?

I decided to tell Eamon when he came home at lunchtime. But I'd have to go out and buy meat for our dinner, in between contractions. I peeled the potatoes and veg while my underwear dried in front of our two-bar electric fire. I checked my watch every time I got a pain, and reckoned I had twenty minutes to get to the shop and back. Throwing my coat on, I hurried from our bedsit at the bottom of the Malahide Road. The friendly butcher knew me well.

'What can I do you for today, Mrs Brady?'

'Four slices of lamb's liver please.'

He threw some slivers on the weighing scales.

'And when's that baby of yours due?'

'Soon.'

He handed me my bill, and just as I proffered the two and six pence through the glass-fronted booth, a whopper of a contraction began to creep up my body.

I managed to walk stiffly out the door.

Oh no! maybe the book was wrong. Was I going to have my baby right here, outside the butcher's opposite Fairview Park?

I pretended to examine my little parcel of meat, and forced myself to take a deep breath to smother the thumping of my heart. Mercifully, the pain began to subside, and I shuffled back around the corner to the safety of our home.

Although bent double most of the time, I managed to cook the dinner, and laid the tiny Formica table for two.

Hurry Eamon, hurry.

At last, windblown, young and handsome, he clumped up the stairs and in the door.

'Hiya, love. Smells good. Any news?'

BIRTH DAYS

As Eamon deposited my case in the hall of the nursing home – it was really a large private house – I asked the midwife could he come upstairs with me to the labour room.

She was a tiny five-foot powerhouse of a lady, with short, wild, wavy hair, a cigarette stuck at the side of her mouth.

'Of course not. That's no place for a man.'

She sounded shocked. Opening the front door, she turned to Eamon and said in a firm voice.

'You can ring in about four hours time, Mr Brady.'

So I was alone – in an ordinary bedroom-like room, frightened and ignorant about the waves of pain that consumed my young body. The nurse popped her head in from time to time.

'Hold on to the bar at the top of the bed, or you'll fall out,' she advised. 'You're doing fine – I'm going to call the doctor now.'

By twenty past nine, just as I felt as if I was tearing in two, the doctor announced loudly, 'You have a fine baby boy – seven pounds, seven ounces.'

I had kept my eyes firmly shut.

But when I looked – the wonder – this roundy, red-faced, plump little son that Eamon and I had conceived, so perfect. We decided to name him after St Ciarán.

'Why are you calling him after Kieran Moore?' Mammy asked crossly, next day. He was a handsome Irish film star, with thick wavy hair. Our new baby had masses of black curly hair too.

When visiting was over, the nurse bustled into the tiny room, handed me a bowl of water, some cotton wool, and my bawling, hungry son.

'If you're going to feed him yourself, you'd better get on with it.' Her tone was brisk.

All the babies in the nursing home were bottle-fed. Breast-feeding was not encouraged. It did not suit her routine. She turned and left me alone.

I couldn't manage to satisfy Ciarán, so I joined him in a crying duet.

The door opened and the nurse strode over to us, handed me a baby's bottle and, without speaking, exited. The bottle worked a treat.

I was not to breastfeed any of my seven children after that, much to Mammy's disapproval.

'I fed all my babies myself, for the first weeks,' she informed me, several times.

I remembered one incident when we were living in Laytown and Marian was the baby. I happened to open the door to the front room. Mam held the baby at her breast. 'Get out! Get out!' she roared at me. Hurriedly, I quit the room.

I stayed in the nursing home for seven days. One afternoon, the nurse summoned me to the nursery. The babies were all in their cots.

'Deirdre, I know you are going to make a good mother, but you are very nervous. Now watch this.' She spread one hand on my baby Ciarán's head, then lifted him up by his skull bones. He dangled and flayed at the air with his pudgy arms and legs, scarlet-faced.

'You see? Babies are not that delicate.'

I was twenty-one years old.

We had nowhere to live when we left the nursing home. Our house in Artane was not yet built. Mrs Brady said we could stay with her. She had a family of eight living in a two-bedroomed house, yet we were welcome. It never occurred to any of us, that Mammy and Daddy could offer us a room in Clontarf – a much bigger, roomier house.

On a grey November afternoon, when I walked into the Brady's house, the parlour fire was blazing, and a sofa-bed made up. On the mirror above the mantelpiece, written in lipstick, were the words, 'Welcome home, baby Ciarán.'

Down in the main room, a bottle of port and a fruitcake were laid out on the table.

'For the ladies only,' Mrs Brady explained.

Two years and four months later, I was back again in the nursing home one Saturday afternoon.

'What's keeping this baby, Deirdre? I have tickets for the rugby final today,' my doctor asked, as I made little progress.

I was aware of the nurse pouring some anaesthetic liquid over my nose and mouth. I knew nothing else, until I awoke, flat on my back, alone, in the same bed by the window. I tried to raise my head to see if my bump was still there. No use. I couldn't even raise my arms. Helpless, I called out for the nurse – over and over.

'What's all the shouting for?' she was standing over me.

'I just wanted to know… Did I have my baby…or did I not…and if I did…is it all right?…and what is it?' Words jumbled in a crush of anxiety.

'You've had another boy, much smaller than your first. He's fine. A bit jaundiced. You'll see him soon enough.'

She stuck a cigarette into my mouth, then swished out the door.

That night I was moved into my own room, and saw my six-pound, seven-ounce baby for the first time. He had scraggy tufts of fine hair, and was bright yellow.

'He looks so tiny,' Eamon said when he saw him. 'I think he was premature.'

We decided to christen him Paraic, as it was near to St Patrick's Day.

'You should name him Horatio,' the doctor suggested, when he called to check on us.

Nelson's Pillar had just been blown up.

My head wasn't right for a long time after the birth. I cried a lot, had no energy, and even forgot the poor little scrap the day we departed the nursing home – left him dressed, lying on the bed upstairs.

Back home, I couldn't do anything – cooking, housework – I just managed to feed the fractious little baby. My kind neighbour, Pat, carried the Moses basket downstairs for me every morning, dressed and minded toddler Ciarán, while I sat and cried. My niece, Marguerite, called to do the housework, and Eamon cooked the dinner when he got home from work.

I remember clearly the loneliness and terror of knowing that I was not in my right mind. One night, Eamon washed my hair for me at the kitchen sink, then sat down by the fire to read his paper. As I tried to wind rollers into my soppy hair, I whispered to myself, 'Now Deirdre, keep your eyes on Eamon all the time, and you won't go mad.'

Another afternoon, Dad happened to call. I had been trying to put a curtain hook back up on the rail. It had been bothering me for days and days. I opened the front door wide to him. 'Daddy… I did it at last… I put the hook back.' I sobbed with elation.

I cried when the baby was asleep, because I knew he was going to wake up crying. I cried when he cried – because he was crying. I was terrified of darkness falling, couldn't sleep, and had no appetite. I went back to my doctor for the six-week check-up.

'And how have you been, Deirdre?' he enquired pleasantly.

I tried to explain what I'd been through.

'You silly girl. You should have come to see me sooner. You have been suffering from post-natal depression, a recognised illness nowadays.'

If only I'd known. I had been afraid to go out. Afraid I'd be put away for being insane.

Pregnant for the third time, I booked into a proper nursing home. The first one had been closed down, and the nurse struck off the register.

Eamon managed to find the money – he said I deserved the bit of spoiling I got – for a private room, good food, and plenty of rest. This time I begged the two midwives not to give me anything to ease my labour. Every time I got a contraction, I would almost faint with the pain. 'We can give you something, Deirdre,' they urged kindly.

'No. Nothing. Please, please,' I moaned.

So baby Eoin had a completely natural childbirth – a placid, black-haired, seven-pound little boy. His hair fell out over his first six months, to be replaced by a soft blond down. I was well and happy that Christmas after his birth, proud of his delivery, even though I roared at the top of my voice as he was born.

When I told our healthy sons that I was expecting again, I was afraid to hope for a girl. I'd had the names Roísín, Catherine, and Catherine again, all ready for the first three times, and they all turned out to be boys. This time I was taking no chances.

When we said night prayers together, the lads would add, 'and bless baby Conor in Mammy's tummy.'

On a Sunday in October, we went for a walk down the Bull Island, then on to Mrs Brady's for tea. I felt a few strongish cramps, so we decided to check with the nurse on the way home. She examined me while Eamon waited outside in the car with the boys. It was nearly seven o'clock.

'You can go home. Deirdre's in labour. Ring me in an hour or so,' she instructed Eamon, much to all our surprise.

He drove the short journey home, and as he was walking in the gate, our neighbour, Pat, came out to congratulate him on his new baby! We had no phone then, and had given the nurse Pat's number.

It was really quick. I had just lit a cigarette (in the delivery room!) when the contractions went into fast forward. The nurse took it from between my fingers as I gasped with shock. At twenty past seven I heard her say, 'You have a baby daughter. Well done.' A daughter – not a 'baby girl' – a 'daughter'!

I was overjoyed, though taken aback a little when I examined my long, skinny, completely baldy baby. Eamon was back again in record time, and we just looked at our daughter in disbelief.

That night I felt a little sad – for imaginary baby Conor. We had no girl's name; all our previous choices had been taken. My sister Marian sent us a telegram. 'Congratulations on your baby *cailín*,' it said. That was it. Cailín Maureen was to be our daughter's name.

The next little chap, Dónal, decided to come into this world the wrong way round. We wondered what his eyes looked like for the first three days – his tiny face was so scrunched up, none were visible. But he unfolded gently, and was a perfect, undemanding baby.

When our second daughter arrived, the doctor announced. 'You have a baby boy, Deirdre. No. Sorry – it's a girl!'

Máiréad was a pretty, black-haired, dark-eyed doll, with a red nose for the first few weeks. A smiling, sociable little girl, she loved attention. Still does!

She was born in January. There were no other patients in the nursing home – the nurse was phasing out the end of her career and was closing down. I had a huge room to myself, with a radio and a fire. I was asked each day what I would like for dinner, then the nurse would go shopping for my choice. Mrs Brady bought me sweet-scented fresias, and Máiréad and I were content in our luxury for seven whole days.

Luxury was not the word to describe my last delivery. I was thirty-eight years old and my doctor advised I attend a maternity hospital. I queued with the other mothers-to-be, young enough to be my daughters, and was examined by a different physician each visit.

The final irony of my child-bearing days occurred when the nurse asked Eamon if he wished to stay with me throughout the labour and delivery.

But it was years too late for us.

He went home to look after the other six children, while I gave birth to our youngest child, Clare, in sterile, impersonal surroundings. This time, I kept my eyes open.

Three days later, as I prepared to leave, I washed my hair and spied my first grey hair.

MISHAP

Eamon, baby Ciarán and I moved from Mrs Brady's to a bedsit in an old house that was being renovated.

The front room was our bedroom and living room. The other dark room had no window. One half had floorboards, on which stood our cooker and washing machine. Where the rest of the floor should have been, there was a sheer drop to a deep black abyss. I would throw the empty cans and cartons down into its mysterious depths.

When cooking, I would listen to my precious transistor, which was balanced on the lid of our dancing washing machine. One day, the transistor fell into the machine and got soaked. I placed it in the oven to dry, but its innards melted. Without much hope, I brought it to a man in Ballybough who fixed electrical goods. Lo and behold, he brought it back to life, and we enjoyed many more years together, until technology overtook us.

UNWELCOME GUESTS

Eamon and me, driving from Dublin to County Clare, nonstop. Seven children jumbled in the back of our old blue Opal Estate. Another scorching day. We are all hot and sweaty, baby Clare fractious, the boys squabbling, thirsty, piled together with our baggage – nine black plastic bags – one for each member.

We reach Lahinch. Another mile to go. We stop the car and hang out the windows to admire the lively Atlantic Sea. A chorus of 'Let's have a swim!' from the children. There are no dissenters. Tumbling out, down the steps, we charge into the cool green sea – me in my dress, the kiddies in their shorts and skirts. Eamon dips little Clare's toes in the foamy water. She squeaks with wonder.

Half an hour later, back in the car, soppy, sandy, and starving! We sit outside the chipper, watching and waiting noisily, as Eamon joins the queue. Shouts of 'Hurrah!' when he emerges, laden down. The fish and chips are gobbled up, elbows and knees stuck in faces, chips on floor, seats wet, vinegar smell. All happy.

Drive on, out past higgledy fields divided by low, careless stone walls, to the old lodge. Stubbornly superior to the dormer bungalows that have begun to spring up, its three storeys stand tall in its isolation. The now shabby three-foot thick walls have ensured its longevity. The sheds that once housed a coach and horse lie derelict behind it.

There are creepy-crawlies in the tap water (piped up from a stream behind the house) and no electricity. A short somewhere. It's almost dark. We dump the (unpacked) bags in the parlour and make up a huge bed on the floor for the children; they won't venture up to the bedrooms in the blackout.

Eamon, Clare and I squeeze into a musty bed that dips in the middle in a tiny room opposite the front door. I lie there squinting at the thick darkness inside and outside.

I can hardly bear the sound of the unfamiliar quiet until a scratching under the floorboards assures me we're not alone.

'Eamon!' I shake his comatose body. 'I'm not staying here. We're going home tomorrow!'

Next morning the sun shines again. We stay.

He is such a good little boy. Playing out the back. Quiet and content. All on his own.

Three-year-old Dónal.

I peep out the kitchen window. He is sitting on the concrete path, his back firm against the shed wall. He is talking. Soft, bossy words. Engrossed with his game.

'No. Not yu' tu'n yet. Come back. Stay aside me.'

I have to find out. I step out into his sunny world.

Stretched out beside his scruffy, healthy, tanned legs is an assortment of worms.

Fat ones, purple ones, half ones, pink ones, mucky ones.

He pats a clear space beside him.

'Do you want to play with my 'wummons' Mammy? They're doing a race.'

BETWEEN

While Eamon and I were raising our ever-increasing family, the lives of my sisters and brothers receded into the background of my world.

Gráinne flitted between Dublin and London working as a first-class secretary. Dark and attractive, perfectly made-up, always dressed in the latest fashion. She eventually settled in Dublin, married and had three children: fair Roísín and Ronán and dark, lanky Rory. Gráinne was gifted with a beautiful voice and an eloquent vocabulary. 'Gráinne will always use ten words where two will do,' Nuala observed dryly.

Nuala was forging ahead, careerwise, based in London, working and travelling for the BBC. She popped over to Dublin now and then. On one particular visit to Clontarf, I can see her clearly, standing in the middle of the green carpet, having an animated discussion with Daddy. She was wearing a tight, finely knitted short dress, nipped in at the waist. The most expensive stylish high heels. Shapely legs. Long golden brown hair – she had it wrapped and straightened each week in London. One hand supporting the elbow of the other arm, a long cigarette stuck between her fingers, waving her hand about to emphasise a point.

Terry was now in the hotel business, travelling and working as a manager, with his wife Trudi, the love of his life. She was slim and attractive, with creamy white skin, long golden hair, and a great sense of fun.

Terry and Trudi had split up before he went away to sea. Trudi was younger than Terry, and his future was uncertain. Some time after returning to Dublin, Terry, who was now in the hotel business, found out where Trudi was working. One December evening, when Trudi had finished work, he just *happened* to be standing in Harcourt Street waiting for the red light to change, when – across the road, at the opposite lights – there stood Trudi. He asked her to join him for a coffee. She did. And for the rest of their lives too.

Don was serving with the British Army all over the world. When he visited Ireland with his three stunningly beautiful children, we were instructed not to mention his job. There were certain places in Dublin which were off limits for a get together with him. When Don visited, he was desperate for Dad's approval. Loud and hyper, he cracked jokes about the army, told of his wealth and earnings. The harder he tried, the more embarrassed and impatient Dad became.

Don went to enormous trouble to get a rare black-and-white photo of Dad conducting a symphony orchestra, blown up, mounted and expensively framed. (Dad had been asked by a photographer from a newspaper what he would like to have been if he hadn't been a journalist, and this picture was the result.)

Don's present was eventually hung in the lobby of the flat.

Meanwhile, back in Clontarf, Marian had been mitching from school. Later, Marian told me that she would set off in the morning at the usual time and head for town, where her friend Jackie lived with her mother Leland in a basement flat. She would hide away down there until school was over.

Nobody at home noticed. Leland had an open home – everyone was welcome. 'One day,' Marian recalled, 'I spied Nuala's legs coming down the metal staircase outside the basement window. Leland and she were good friends. It didn't take her long to figure out what I was doing there.'

Nuala spoke to Dad, and told him about a well-known learned man she knew, Gus Martin, who had recommended a boarding school in Thurles.

One summer day, Dad summoned Marian. 'Daughter, we're going on a little trip. Have you something nice to wear?' Off in the car they went to Thurles, arriving at the parlour of the boarding school, where they drank tea with the kindly nuns. 'We hear you haven't been doing too well?' one of them said to her. 'But you'll work hard here.'

And study hard, for one whole year, Marian did, achieving the necessary honours for a degree in Trinity College.

Noreen had moved to London by then. With the girls gone, young Dermot spent most of his time down the Bull Wall, sometimes fishing, sometimes hanging about with unsavoury pals. Cycling home across the wooden planks of the bridge, his bike got stuck one day. He had a nasty fall, and lost his front tooth. Barely fifteen, he had to get a false tooth.

He came to stay with us in Rush for a few days. One summer evening he set off for the town with Eamon's two teenage sisters. 'Be back by eleven!' I warned them. 'And no drinking.' They arrived back on the dot. Dermot gave me a big smile. I saw the gap in his mouth. 'Where's your tooth?'

They had to tell the truth. They had indeed been drinking and, on their way home along the beach, Dermot had got sick. 'Out you go,' I said to the three sheepish youngsters, and don't come back without Dermot's tooth.' Somehow they found it in a pool of vomit back along the dark dunes.

When Dermot started to get into 'trouble' in Clontarf, he was escorted over to London on the ferry.

Now there was just Niamh, Mam and Dad left in Clontarf.

Dad announced that he was selling the house – it was too big and expensive to maintain. They were moving to a new ground-floor flat nearby. Mam was aghast; she had made such a huge effort to own her only home, now it was back to renting again. But she was powerless against his reasonableness.

Dad had Brown Thomas's measure and fit the curtains and carpets, and bought new beds and furniture. He arranged for a cleaning lady to come once a week to the flat, sent his shirts and sheets to the Swan Laundry and, on his days off, he did the cooking.

Niamh attended Mount Temple School. She had a great ear for music – she could whistle a whole symphony by the time she was eleven. In her early teens she spent a lot of time with our family. She came to Rush with us in the summer, St Anne's Park on Sundays, and had a joint sixteenth-birthday disco with Ciarán (when he was only thirteen!) in our front room. I remember that, everytime I checked, the lights were out.

Mam settled into a routine of visiting her local, meeting her friends there. She had two or three loyal friends. Reading her books – mostly in bed. Hair done each Friday. Sometimes she went off with Dad to a hotel or a posh reception, but she was never comfortable in public.

THE YARD

It seemed like a good plan at the time.

After Mr Brady died, the males of the clan took over the running of his business in a walled-off space with high gates, underneath the railway arches in Spring Garden Street. Mr Brady had been brought up there, in a little cottage, tucked under one of the arches. His father had worked on the railway, and had been given the home and yard by the Great Northern Railway Company.

The Brady brothers pooled their money, stocked up on supplies – bags of potatoes, vegetables, eggs, fruit, sand and gravel, logs, turf and Kosangas cylinders. They bought an old Volkswagen open-backed lorry for deliveries. The youngest son looked after the business during weekdays.

One of the brothers or the grandsons took over on Saturday, the busiest day. Or exchanged shifts. It was all pretty informal. Whoever was in charge sat in front of the gas fire beside the kettle, and wrote everything down in the accounts book.

'My first job was to feed the dogs who lived in, and guarded, the yard,' Eoin recalled. 'Mrs Brady cooked the mixture in a large pot. I had to collect it and carry it over to them. The smell was terrible. The dogs were huge, and starving. If they hadn't been chained, they would have eaten me as well.'

Then to the business of the business. Top of the agenda? A cup of tea. Kettle boiled. Cups emptied. Time to get stuck in to work.

Kosangas cylinders and four-stone bags of spuds to be lugged up steps. Deliveries and collections of money owed. Lunch break. Chips from the chipper around the corner. Little old ladies who dropped in for their weekly chat. A tea break. Trips to the bookies. To the shops for jaffa cakes, or the paper. If a relative drops in, the kettle is filled again. Then wages to be sorted. Suppliers to be paid. All entered into the book, of course. Incoming orders, monies received, cash paid out, more cash paid out, followed by even more cash out.

Afternoon tea break. Essential.

'We had a wireless with no knobs. It had to be turned on with a pliers, then took five minutes to warm up. There were two old dears who lived locally who would call in at the same time every week to have a dance to the music before buying their few messages,' Ciarán remembered.

'Then there was an old bachelor, Paddy Moore, always impeccably dressed in a fedora hat, suit and tie. He'd ask for half a head of cabbage, and for us to keep the other half for him until the next Saturday.'

One December, someone came up with the idea of buying a lorry load of Christmas trees to sell. By January there were still about fifty left – going cheap.

Our family never had to buy potatoes or logs. Eamon brought our supplies home each Saturday evening. I'm sure it all was noted down in 'the book'.

For over a year, the yard in Spring Garden Street buzzed with life on a Saturday. A social centre, where faithful old customers unloaded their worries, shared a joke and a laugh. A bookie's paradise. A drop-in centre for friends and relatives. If your name was Brady (and you were not female), you had a vested interest in it.

But it was a case of two many chiefs, too many Indians, and not enough money to go round, that eventually caused the demise of the yard.

CINDERFELLAS

Once upon a time there were two brothers who, on finishing school, went off to their Debs' Ball. The first to go was Ciarán, who had been working during the summer, and had some money put aside. The following year was Paraic's turn, but he was stony-broke. But they each looked splendid on their respective big nights. From the top of their number - two haircuts, down to their black shiny shoes and their penguin suits, there was no discernable difference.

But there was. Just look at what it cost each of them:

Ciarán

Tickets:	£ 28
Hairstyle, city saloon:	£ 5
Three-piece suit, bought especially:	£ 80
Shirt:	£ 10
Shoes:	£ 20
Socks:	£ 2
Dicky bow:	£ 4
Corsage, local florist:	£ 6
Chocs:	£ 10
Taxis, to hotel and home again:	£ 20
Photos, two:	£ 20
Drinks, several:	£ 20
Total:	£225

Paraic

Tickets:	£	30
Haircut, courtesy of the ma:	£	0
Jacket, black wool, sale of work, dry-cleaned:	£	3
Trousers, borrowed big brother's:	£	0
Shirt, birthday shirt, washed and ironed:	£	0
Shoes, the da's:	£	0
Dicky bow, the granda's:	£	0
Socks, new!:	£	2
Corsage, red rose and fern from garden:	£	0
Chocs, small box:	£	4
Taxis, uncle's car there, CIE bus home at 9 a.m.:	£	1
Photos, none after seeing big brother's:	£	0
Drinks, few:	£	10
Total:	£	50

And they both lived happily ever after!

HURT

I noticed little Máiréad was walking with a slight limp when I collected her from Junior Infants class on Friday.

'Did you hurt your leg in school today?'

'No, I didn't. Teacher asked me did I fall down at home.'

We stopped on the path. I felt her soft plump leg. Not a mark anywhere.

'Are your shoes hurting you?'

'No.'

She let go of my hand and skipped ahead, plaits swinging. A small chubby figure in her sky-blue smock, dark eyes twinkling in her rosy, heart-shaped face.

But there was something not right about her gait.

I was worried. Eamon and I had arranged to go away for the weekend to a wedding in County Clare.

'Maybe we shouldn't go. I don't want to leave the boys minding Máiréad if it's something serious,' I said to Eamon when he came home from work.

'We'll be back on Sunday. If she's still limping, you can bring her to the doctor on Monday morning. She probably banged it somewhere and the bruise hasn't come up yet.'

I felt reassured, and agreed with him.

So off we went to the wedding in peaceful County Clare. Spacious skies and hilly fields, wild daffodils sprouting up in abundant clumps.

Cailín, now twelve, came with us. She wore make-up for the first time. The reception was a huge affair, the dance floor packed for each set dance. Around six o'clock most of the men disappeared for an hour or so – the cows had to be milked.

When we arrived home on Sunday night, Ciarán and Paraic were waiting up for us. The other children were all in bed. Ciarán, usually so jolly, looked very serious.

'Máiréad's leg seemed to get worse, so I brought her down to the doctor on my bike on Saturday afternoon.'

Paraic interrupted breathlessly. 'The doctor wasn't there and I told Ciarán to bring her to the hospital, but he wouldn't. He said he'd wait till you got home.'

I hurried upstairs and looked at my sleeping little people. Máiréad and Clare were heaped together in slumber, Máiréad's black hair tangled across her hot face. Dónal, straight and untossed in the bottom bunk, and Eoin, not quite asleep.

'Did you have a good time?' he whispered down from the top bunk. 'I'm glad you're home. We missed you.'

Next morning Eamon brought Máiréad straight to Temple Street Hospital. At eleven o'clock, my neighbour Pat came in to our hall.

'Eamon wants you on the phone. I'll mind the kids.'

I raced into her house and grabbed the phone, shaking.

'Di, can you come into the hospital? Ask Pat to mind the children. Máiréad has something called osteomyelitis. It's very serious.'

Torrents of guilt, fear and panic were pushed aside when I saw my smiling, brave little daughter, a drip in her arm.

'It doesn't hurt, Ma.'

The doctors explained how the disease had manifested itself in

Máiréad's knee, but thanks to powerful new drugs, it could be arrested and even cured.

She wore a cast for six weeks, took her medicine without complaint, and attended school – I pushed her in Clare's buggy. She was the sunniest, bravest little patient.

Thank God she made a complete recovery.

The guilt still lingers though.

WILL YE NO COME BACK AGAIN

Eoin rang to tell us he'd be up in Dublin from college in Limerick over the weekend. Could we put up a few friends from the athletic club overnight?

Naturally we said yes. In our large family, a few more would hardly be noticed.

However, we were slightly taken aback when a coach – complete with a trailer – pulled up outside our small, terraced house. Two figures emerged from the bus: Eoin and the driver. They proceeded to unhitch the trailer, leaving it at our gate. Then, to our relief, the driver took his coach away.

A big hello smile on his face for us, Eoin began to bring the contents of the trailer – holdalls, running gear, jackets, sleeping bags – into the hall until there was only climbing space left.

With a hasty hug, he said, 'Must dash back into town to meet the team – there's a dance arranged. I'm afraid we won't be back home till twoish.'

DEIRDRE BRADY

'How many is "we"?' I called after his agile figure, as he clambered over the luggage on his way out.

'About nineteen.'

We already had our nephew, Aran from Colorado, staying with us, so we now had a grand total of thirty humans who would need sleep that night! Our two eldest girls were dispatched to their aunt's, and the smaller children tucked into the ends of big brothers' and cousins' beds. The remaining eighteen would share the box room, sitting and dining rooms, sleeping in armchairs and on floors.

At half one in the morning, Eamon and I retired to our precious double bed, leaving a large chicken stew and some bed covers handy. We lay awake until the quietness of the night was exploded by the chatter and laughter of the gang as they approached our house. We relaxed then, lulled to sleep by the rhythmic sounds of the bathroom door opening and shutting, and the constant flush of the loo.

Awakening on Sunday morning, our bedroom was an oasis in the middle of a mad house, bursting at the seams from the noise of voices, stereo, footsteps thumping up and down the stairs to the perpetually busy bathroom.

Half an hour later, still in bed, we feared we'd never get a turn. Urged on by the call of nature, I made a dash for it, only to confront two girls washing their hair. Muttering apologies, I scurried back to the safety of my room to resume my vigil. Twenty minutes later, taking advantage of a gap in the traffic, washed and dressed, I ventured downstairs.

Elbowing my way through tall athletic bodies in the kitchen, in a desperate attempt to get a mug of tea, I was spotted by Eoin, who introduced me to the smiling girls and boys.

At midday, a voice in the hall shouted, 'Everybody for Limerick, the coach is outside!'

All too quickly, Eamon and I were standing at the gate, waving goodbye to the invigorating youngsters. They had washed all the dishes and tidied places they hadn't even untidied. As we walked back inside our neat and quiet home, it seemed surprisingly spacious.

LET'S GET AWAY FROM IT ALL

'Summertime and the Livin' is Easy'. For our family of nine, it's a two-month holiday in a wooden shanty by the sea.

But 'It Ain't Necessarily So', because, at the same time, my seven brothers and sisters-in-law, their seven spouses, plus a total of twenty-four children, five dogs and three cats, pack up and head for the same place.

For the first few days, there are eight separate families: polite, well mannered. Kiddies are kind to cousins, say their prayers, brush teeth, share buckets and spades. But as time goes by, we gradually merge into one huge, disorganised, mad, noisy commune – all traces of civilised living erased. Toothbrushes are walked into the sand, faces left unwashed. If a child is naughty, punishment is doled out by whichever mother happens to be nearby.

Quarrels between husband and wife become public property. The women close ranks, while the husbands disappear as often as possible.

A typical day follows:

Awake to the usual morning sounds. Patter of rain on the felt-covered roof, toddlers squabbling outside my window, dogs barking at the terrified milkman delivering a full crate of milk bottles, on the hill behind the hut. Distant tumbling of waves.

My sandy eyes open. The familiar words 'This side up. Fragile.' stamped in black, look down on me from the ceiling which has been constructed out of wooden pallets.

Breakfast time is everyone for themselves, and the motto, first come, first eat, rules OK.

Coffee break for the holiday mums follows before, during, and after breakfast, with an indepth discussion.

'What meat will we buy for dinner?'

'How about bacon?'

'My kids won't eat bacon.'

'I'd love a piece of steak.'

'We can't afford it.'

'It will have to be mince again.'

'And beans. The kids love beans.'

'We had beans yesterday.'

Silence.

'I need cigarettes.'

'Me too.'

'So do I.'

Get me forty.'

'OK. First item on the shopping list: one hundred and fifty cigarettes.'

After an hour or so of hard mental slogging, the list is ready for the husband of the day to drive into the village. Eight sighs of relief.

Now for the kettle brigade. First up that morning gets the kettle to do her washing. As we only have five clothes lines, there is a waiting list. It's not uncommon to find that a thoughtful sister-in-law has taken in your laundry and left it nice and damp – ready for ironing – on your bed.

The rest of us relax in the sunshine, if it visits us, and keep an eye on the thirty-two children while we peel the four-stone bag of potatoes for the evening meal.

Decide to have soup and salad – again – for lunch. No big problem here, except what flavour soup today?

A swim is squeezed in if there's enough sea vacant.

By this time the exhausted husband has arrived back with the mountain of groceries, left the change on the table, and fled to the nearest pub. The kiddies are each handed a dripping ice-pop. This keeps them quiet for a few minutes, so the ladies can have their afternoon meeting to sort out finances.

This is not an easy task. We can't split everything eight ways. Smokers, amount of children, husbands, dogs, and babies have to be added and subtracted. Most of us find an urgent job to do just then, and leave May, our financial wizard, surrounded by scraps of paper, cash and ash.

The highlight of the day at last. Dinner. No trouble. Our chain-gang system works smoothly.

Strongest mum stands at the cooker, and dishes out portions of meat onto plates held by second-in-command. She passes same to number three mum for vegetables and potatoes. Then down the line to number four for mashing, buttering, or sauce. The rest of the team's duties include wiping noses, keeping kids quiet, picking up spoons and forks from the sandy floor, stopping fights and refilling spilt drinks.

Small kids, pregnant females and working men are fed first. Before they have time to ask for seconds, their plates are whisked away from under their noses and sent back up the line to be washed, dried, and filled for the starving second-sitting gang.

Dinner over – the men are left to clean up, hopefully – and the most important meeting of the day takes place.

Topic? Babysitting.

This is worked out depending on who wishes to go out that night (everybody), who has been asked out by their husbands (nobody), and how often they have been out already this week (as often as possible). The lucky ones rush to find their respective children, put them to bed (in theory), get dolled up, and vamoose.

It may not be everybody's idea of a holiday. There's no peace and quiet, privacy, rest, or choice of food, but we can all have that when we return to our own homes.

After all, a change is as good as a rest, isn't it?

A blue sea of sky, bordered by feathery leaves of trees on both sides above me, as I cycle along Mount Prospect Avenue this sunny Saturday morning.

Turning in towards the flat, the windows and front door are wide open and I can hear Dad's music pouring out. It's Beethoven's Pastoral Symphony. *Perfect choice for this perfect day.*

Dad is half seated on the edge of a chair – reading the sleeve notes of a record – freshly shaved, shirt sleeves rolled up neatly, casual cream trousers. He looks up as I walk in, all smiles for me. Such a warm welcome. I have come to use his phone – to book a holiday house in Donegal for our family. He lowers the volume right down, but I say, 'Can we wait till it finishes?'

We listen together as the sunlight stripes the green carpet, until the final strains fade out.

SOMEBODY SPECIAL

'Mam. Brian-Thomas is here!'

Ten-year-old Clare ran out to the gate ahead of me. I could see Brian-Thomas Hardiman's pale little face peering out the window of the red minibus. As the smiling lady slid open the side door, he half hid his head in the crook of his elbow, chuckling and beaming with delight and shyness to see us again. I lifted his slight bony frame from the bus. Excitedly, he grasped Clare's hand, barely reaching her shoulder, even though he was fifteen. Pulling her with him, he loped up the path and on into our house, as familiar to him now as his own home.

Brian-Thomas is one of God's special children. He has learning difficulties. He comes to stay with us for short breaks throughout the year, thanks to the Breakaway programme.

Three years previously, a poster caught my attention, showing a chubby, smiling Down Syndrome toddler whizzing down a slide. The caption said something like 'Would you give this child a holiday in your home?' The address was St Michael's House in Glasnevin, a centre that cares for people with special needs.

I thought about our seven healthy children and how fortunate we had been. After talking it over with Eamon, I sent off a letter. A social worker called to chat with us first, and subsequently we were invited to attend a Breakaway course, along with other prospective couples.

It was during these informal talks we discovered how little we knew about children with learning difficulties. I, for one, had a lot of misconceptions.

Firstly, the idea behind Breakaway is to give the parents a rest, not the child. Children like Brian-Thomas are happy most of the time, as long as they are cared for and loved. Few parents ever have a holiday, or even a weekend break, on their own or with the rest of their family.

Secondly, as Eamon pointed out, 'You don't just take a child for a holiday, then drop the whole idea.'

He was right. This is a big commitment.

Our afternoon visit to St Michael's in Raheny had a profound effect on us. Some of the children had both severe physical and mental disabilities. Yet the atmosphere was so happy, with volunteers and staff lavishing care and affection on each child.

In the special school, mildly handicapped children like Brian-Thomas, who can walk, but not talk; eat, but have no teeth, are encouraged to reach their full potential.

As we learned more, one thing became apparent to us both. We were not going to be able to choose a child ourselves. Each has unique difficulties. The experienced staff would match the child to the host parents. At the end of the course, if the couple still wish to go ahead, and if St Michael's decide they are suitable to join the Breakaway programme, a one-year contract is signed by three parties: the child's parents, St Michael's, and the host couple.

Brian-Thomas was assigned to us, and we considered ourselves very lucky.

Introductions were made gradually – a meeting first, an afternoon visit, then an overnight stay – to help everyone get to know one another. It was comforting to have St Michael's back-up. Each child has a social worker who organises everything, and they are

127

always available to sort out any problems.

We were able to take Brian-Thomas for one week each year, and a couple of weekends. We met his family, who love him dearly. He is their youngest.

'When you take Brian-Thomas, we just relax and have a lie-in,' his mother, Marie, told us. They don't go away anywhere themselves. 'By the end of the week we miss him and can't wait to see him home.'

The first time Brian-Thomas stayed overnight with us, we were nervous wrecks, even though we had been well prepared. We showered him with attention, and crept round the house once we had got him to bed. The responsibility was frightening!

Now we look forward to him coming. We've grown very fond of him, and are familiar with all his little ways.

His mischievous giggle, his habit of running around in a circle, his fascination for buses – toy ones and real ones. He's very clever, and has been taught basic sign language in school. We know all the important ones – drink, biscuit, Mam, Dad, bed (he never wants to go!) and thanks. He's funny too, demands piles of attention, and looks like a little old man when he sucks in his gums.

He is mad about our young Clare.

Squeezed tight beside her on the sofa, he gazes adoringly at the side of her face while she watches television, and waves goodbye in its direction the minute her programme is over. He follows Clare about like a puppy, touching her ponytail, tracksuit, and runners frequently, in mute admiration. He won't go to bed until she does (she pretends), then tucked up with his soother, biscuit, drink, and collection of buses, he waves goodnight to us all.

Of course, it's not all easy. It's no fun being dragged out of a warm bed at seven in the morning on a cold, dark Saturday, by his persistent tugging! He has no conception of time, and signs for his breakfast, a drink, to be dressed, whilst handing me my dressing gown, and pointing to my slippers – all at once!

It's sad too, when the children get fed up with him and he stands forlornly at the gate, watching them play.

But having Brian-Thomas stay with us has enriched our lives. Our friends and relatives, and especially our neighbours, have learned so much about youngsters with learning difficulties – thanks to him. As I watch our children and their friends play so naturally and yet so protectively with him, I think back to the first time he came, and their shy curiosity as they stared at this 'strange' little person.

Now he's just Brian-Thomas to them, accepted for himself, nothing special.

They see the child, not the handicap.

BE IT EVER SO HUMBLE

Welcome to our happy home. A small three-up, two-down terraced house, which has managed to accommodate Eamon, myself and our seven children, on an expanding shoestring.

I know it looks just the same as the houses on either side of us, but come on inside, and I'll show you what an innovative husband and wife can achieve. As the bulk of all income disappears down nine tummies, no cash can be spared for refurbishments or repairs.

Step into the hall. Notice the baldy edges on the stairs' carpet? No? Thanks to the right shade of shoe polish – well rubbed in.

Next stop, the kitchen-cum-dining room. Those varnished presses were constructed by Eamon from wooden pallets he brought home from work. The red velvet lampshade was once our daughter's dress. Rest awhile on the settee – covered with material from two of my large kilts.

What do you think of the fireplace? The mahogany mantle was originally a railway sleeper, the granite stones from a neighbour's discarded rockery, and the hearth is a smashed up marble stand, cemented together.

Unique? Yes, I agree.

Now the sitting room. I bought that Victorian armchair for a fiver and reupholstered it myself. Beneath its elegant outer cover, elastic bands keep the springs together, and an old sack dress replaced the hessian. Those polished works of art on the walls are the older boys' woodwork pieces from school. Take a peek under the frill of that easy chair. The handle of a hammer stands in for the missing leg.

Care to visit the bathroom? Yes, you're right – those are fireplace tiles around the bath. We had some over. They have a tendency to slip into the water when one is having a particularly hot bath.

Certainly. I'll leave you alone for a minute. Be careful though. The toilet seat has been known to fall on the floor. It's on our list. If the loo won't flush properly, don't worry. The large kilt pin replacing the broken spring has probably opened. Also, you might not notice the cork replacing the bung beneath the sink. From a 1984 bottle of wine – a good year.

Okay? Are you ready for the boys' room?

I've just finished painting it. My father-in-law gave me the iron beds. He used them for his hen run – to stop them escaping. After I'd scraped all the hen droppings off, you can see I painted them the same colour as the ceiling and walls. Dusky pink – a special offer. The boys haven't seen it yet. Do you think they'll like it?

And this is our bedroom. You'd never guess that two stout logs have been supporting the end of the double bed for the past ten years, or that Eamon sawed an old dressing table in half to make the bedside presses. That's the mirror part hanging on the wall.

I see you admiring the back garden.

The peculiar shade of paint on the garage? A none too successful brainwave to mix all the scraps of paint we found in the shed – gloss, emulsion, undercoat, bicycle paint – with a dash of water and white spirits.

The faded blue deck-chair covering was once Eamon's denim jacket. Our rustic trellis fence was hewn from the branches of our cypress trees.

You don't see any trees?

131

Unfortunately they had to be chopped down after they went on fire. Oh yes. Huge sheets of flame shooting up in to the wintry sky. Terrible. We were asleep of course.

Must you leave so quickly? But you haven't seen the girls' room yet...

EXPOSED

The tap of pebbles smacking against my bedroom window dragged me half awake from my deep, comfy sleep. Saturday morning, early December, about eight o'clock. Sleep-in day for all the family.

I stumbled out of bed and opened the window. Standing beneath me on the back lawn, a neighbour from the row of houses backing our row was gesticulating frantically in the direction of the back lane. I raised my sleepy eyes to look.

Sheets of flame were shooting up the first two conifers along our back wall, crackling into the grey morning sky with a piny smell.

'Our trees are on fire!' I screamed at the comatose Eamon, as I ran past the bed to alert the children.

I grabbed toddler Clare and hurried down to the front room. I couldn't bear to look. I rocked back and forth with her in my arms. I thought of Charlie's garage next to our trees – its Tarmacadam roof. After a while I forced myself to venture into the kitchen. Hiding beneath the windowsill, I observed the scene.

The back garden and lane were filled with neighbours, children, dogs, noise, and hosepipes. Our friend Larry was standing on top of the wall in his pyjamas, holding a garden hose from which trickled a tiny stream of water. Others raced back and forth with buckets and basins, launching the contents up at the trees – soaking the people below – not reaching the merrily galloping flames in the high branches.

The fire brigade arrived and expertly extinguished the flames in twenty minutes. Soppy, blackened tree trunks with denuded branches were left exposed for all to see.

Everyone wanted to know. How had the fire started?

I alone knew the answer. I had figured it out.

Nine-year-old Dónal had built a secret den with his tent in the trees overshadowing my compost heap. I had emptied the ashes from the fire there every day. It was a cold winter, but the ashes had obviously stayed hot, and a corner of Dónal's tent had dropped down and dipped into the compost heap, until it suddenly ignited that windy morning.

I summoned up the courage to claim from our insurance, so that we could compensate our neighbour and have the poor ugly trees felled.

'I'm afraid your trees are not covered for fire insurance. It's not a common occurrence in suburban Dublin.' I was informed gravely.

So I claimed for Dónal's tent and bought him roller-skates to cheer him up.

I stayed in a lot after that.

LETTING GO

It was early autumn. Our large, noisy family, squashed into a small house, struggling along financially, but happy and close-knit. Five schoolgoing children, one toddler, and Ciarán, the eldest at nineteen, with a steady job. He was a fine athlete, trained and raced in his spare time. Unexpectedly, he received a phone call from America. He was offered a four-year athletic scholarship to Wyoming State University.

After much deliberation, he accepted. Eamon and I thought this would be a great opportunity for him to get a degree, but we would miss him so much.

Ciarán was a very happy-go-lucky teenager. His life revolved around his family, his girlfriend Helen, and his running. On payday, his younger brothers and sisters looked forward to seeing his tracksuited figure appear at the door, his backpack bulky with goodies for them. Before doling out the sweets, he'd jokingly check how they had fared in their Friday spelling test at school, amidst lots of tumbling and wrestling on the floor.

A bar of chocolate was placed on top of his generous weekly money, left on the table for me.

There was great excitement at home as letters, important forms and phone calls (from a phone box) sped across the Atlantic. Everything had to be rushed in time for the 'fall' term. The university would pay for his college fees, athletic training and accommodation, but not his airfare. Ciarán's workmates, friends, relations, and our neighbours dazed us with their kindness. They showered him with money, good-luck cards, gifts (which included a Bible and an Aran sweater – there's heavy snow in Laramie, we were told).

Each day rushed past in a haze of preparations, culminating in a huge farewell party at home. Ciarán joked and laughed, and said, 'What can I say?' and we sang 'The Man from Laramie' yet again.

Next morning, the realisation that he was really leaving finally hit us. Ciarán, who had never been abroad before, was saying goodbye to his family, friends, Helen, and his country. We didn't expect to see him again for at least two years, as he would have to work in America the following summer, and wouldn't be able to afford the flight home and back again.

He had grown up in the past few weeks. This solid, cheerful, uncomplicated young man. Grown up and away from us. What should have been a gradual process had been telescoped into this short time. His imminent departure had brought him and his girlfriend closer together, and Eamon and I had seen little of him in those last precious days.

We put his cases with the unfamiliar address in the boot of the car and left the house to see him off for his twelve-hour flight to Colorado. He sat, quiet and still, in the back seat, holding on tightly to Helen's hand.

At the airport, the four of us sat awkwardly and silently in the huge noisy bar. Too soon it was boarding time. We jumped to our feet, wanting to say so much, now that it was too late. This first child of mine, who was nearly a man, hugged each one of us, separately, lovingly.

Then my son, with his black curly hair, his strong stocky figure, the smell of his new Aran sweater still with me, walked away.

SURPRISE

Our older working children had been saving secretly to treat Eamon and me to a holiday for our twenty-fifth wedding anniversary. We chose Hotel Lapad, near Dubrovnik, from a Yugotour brochure. One whole week together alone.

The travel agent explained that Yugo airlines don't fly direct from Dublin. We drove to Belfast in the lashings of rain. It was our first time in an aeroplane! I put my foot down hard on the floor to try to slow the plane down as we sped along the runway.

We arrived at our hotel just after midnight and were ushered to the dining room by a night porter who spoke only Serbo-Croatian. Two side plates with a wrinkled apple on each, served as our evening meal. We finished, rather quickly, and were shown up to our room – crisp white sheets on two single beds, a little balcony overlooking Cruz Bay.

Worn out with excitement and all the travelling, Eamon suggested leaving the unpacking until the morning and I rang down to reception to order breakfast in our room.

'I don't know if they understood me. Nobody seems to speak English.'

We dropped our clothes on the floor, and took a bed each.

Next morning there was a knock, then the door opened, and a tall moustached porter walked into the room. 'Bradley?' he enquired. We nodded together. Immediately he lifted our two suitcases, bowed, then walked out, off down the corridor.

Eamon looked at me. 'What did you say last night? Run after him quick. He thinks we're checking out!'

I was not going to chase after him practically naked, so I grabbed the phone, trying to make someone downstairs understand. Half an hour later, our cases and a tray with a pot of lukewarm water and two cups were delivered to our room!

Of course, we did not know that room service is not included in a package holiday.

During our amazing week we discovered that apples were a rarity, cherries were served with everything: as jam for breakfast, in sauce for dinner and stewed for dessert. The tiny cars were all exactly the same – there was no advertising of any kind – and Tito's picture hung everywhere.

WONDER

We'd come to Medjugorje on a day trip from Dubrovnik. Although Yugoslavia (as it was then) was a communist country, the authorities knew about the young people who claimed they'd seen Our Lady. It brought in much-needed revenue, so they turned a blind eye. Our courier on the hair-raising coach journey – narrow, crumbling roads above precarious abysses – indicated good humouredly that she thought we were all slightly mad.

Medjugorje was a snug little hamlet, nestling in a valley between sheltering hills. Alighting from our coach we were immediately aware of a soothing air of peace and tranquillity. Birds were singing, and women with black aprons and headscarves were bent over working in the lush, green fields. They stopped and smiled at us as we passed them.

We attended an uplifting Mass – said in a myriad of languages – and shook hands with people from Japan, America, Scotland, Italy. In the gorgeous afternoon heat, we climbed the steep hill where the first apparition supposedly took place. Strangers helped each other up the rocky incline, carrying bags for the less agile among us.

Back down near the church again, there was just enough time to purchase some cheap rosary beads, then we headed for the square.

We stood facing a small, plain building. Up the steps, in a little room there, Our Lady was expected to appear to the young visionaries at six o'clock. The square was already packed with hundreds of people, waiting respectfully, talking quietly in different languages.

Suddenly, someone shouted in English, 'Look at the sun!'

Eamon and I had no sunglasses, but instinctively we raised our eyes skywards.

I felt no discomfort as I observed the blazing sun. It spun, swirled, rotated fully in the sky, moving as it twirled, coming closer, then receding, and all around it, shooting from its centre, streams of the most amazing, beautiful colours.

Something made me look over to the cross silhouetted on the hill top. It too had an aura of brilliant lights encircling it.

I don't know how long it lasted, but it was wonderful, frightening, moving. I looked at the faces around me. Had they seen what I'd just seen? Or was I hallucinating? The murmurs that spread through the crowd, the strangers beside me, Eamon's expression, all testified that we had witnessed something supernatural.

Still reeling from the shock, my attention was drawn back to the steps leading up to the apparition room. Over the door was a bare lightbulb. A Franciscan priest would switch this on when Our Lady arrived. Everyone waited, quiet now; only the chorus of birds in the trees could be heard. It was almost six o'clock.

Seconds before the light went on, an eerie silence descended on the square. The birds stopped chirping. There was not a sound.

When the light went off, I dashed back to our waiting coach. Where was Eamon? Paddy last, he joined us. Breathlessly, he plonked downed beside me. 'I couldn't get the rosary beads blessed so I ran back and just touched the bag against the outside wall of the apparition room.

I was not impressed. I put them in my handbag.

Back in the luxury of our hotel room that night, Eamon enquired, 'Where's the bag with the rosary beads?'

Emotionally drained and exhausted, I knew that he had heard stories about rosary beads turning to gold. Impatiently, I emptied the contents on to the bed. They were exactly the same as when we had bought them – cheap silver wire, tiny black beads.

'Satisfied?' I demanded, impatiently. We put them away.

***

Returning home on our Yugo Airlines plane, I could see the white tips of the Alps way below us as we drank our Plavac wine. Our plane landed at Dublin Airport. Naturally, no one had informed us about this. Passengers started to disembark.

'Can we get off too?' I asked the hostess. 'We live twenty minutes from here.'

She examined our ticket. 'No, I'm sorry, your return is to Belfast. We'll be taking off shortly.'

Eamon reminded me that our car was up there too.

So we added about four hours to our journey – getting off at Belfast and driving back to Dublin.

'How come it took us one hour less to fly back to Ireland from Yugoslavia than it did on our flight out?' I asked Eamon, as we booted along the road.

'It was downhill all the way home,' he explained.

Back home to rainy Ireland, and our welcoming children. I gave six-year-old Clare her present of a Yugo Airlines meal – a sealed brown tray with compartments for a roll, jam, cheese, wine, and cutlery, while Eamon opened the paper bag to give the older children a rosary beads each.

The wire of five of the pairs glowed with rich gold links. Why only some? They were all the same. Why not all of them?

We had no answer.

LAST DAY

'Let's pop in to see Angela,' I suggested. She was Eamon's sister. We had spent many holidays together in Rush, and I was very fond of her.

'Is it not too late? It's after twelve.'

'You know she never goes to bed early. We haven't seen her for ages.'

We were in great form – coming from the Pavarotti concert in the Point. It had been a wonderful night, and Angela lived close by in East Wall.

All the lights were on in her house and we got a great welcome. Angela's son Thomas and his fiancée Sonia were there – drinking tea and chatting in the dining room. They had just arrived from London. Tomorrow the whole family was travelling to spend the New Year with Stephen, her eldest son, in Galway.

Two years older than Eamon, Angela was a quiet, self-effacing person. She loved a chat, just like her mother. She home-permed her hair regularly, and washed and set it in hair clips every Saturday night. She had worked as a legal secretary, a highly skilled job, and after her marriage had raised her five children with gentle care.

She spent little money on herself.

When her daughter Carol declared she intended to study accountancy, an ambitious goal for a young girl from a working-class family, Angela supported and helped her with the costs through college. Carol was now working as a fully-fledged accountant.

All Angela's children had chosen original paths. Stephen held an important job in the civil service, Thomas was working as a counsellor in London, Eamon was studying English at Trinity, and Rita was studying Law.

Angela was a bit of a worrier though. 'It's just the way I am. If I didn't have something to worry about, then I'd really be worried,' she told me one time.

Tonight she rattled on good-humouredly about her main concern: the trip tomorrow.

She always spent New Year's Eve at home in Dublin. But she had not seen Stephen's family over the Christmas, and she had lots of wrapped presents to bring. Would there be enough room for them all in Carol's car? Her four-year-old grandson, Jude, wanted to travel with his Nana too. (The others would follow the next evening, in a second car.)

And what should she wear?

Secondly, she had recently gone back on the cigarettes, and was not too happy about it. 'If you enjoy a smoke, what harm is it?' said Eamon.

Carol appeared in the door with her beautiful, dark-eyed little daughter. Emily, just five, was all excited about the prospect of travelling with her cousin Jude. They were the best of pals.

'I'm not staying, Ma. I've still to pack. Will you be ready by eight o'clock tomorrow morning? I want to skip the traffic, it's a long journey. Stephen is going to meet us on the Headford Road. He said we'll never find his house. It's in a remote spot.'

Angela walked us to the door. We wished each other a Happy New Year, and we called 'safe journey tomorrow' to Carol as she got into her car.

After the hectic days of Christmas, New Year's Eve was unusually easy-going for Eamon and me. The children had various plans for that evening, so we would have the house to ourselves. In the afternoon, we visited a dear old friend and returned to a precious, empty home. We were going to stay put, and I was looking forward to going set dancing on New Year's Day.

'I'm going to make us chips and eggs for a change,' Eamon promised. We'd had enough turkey variations.

'We should catch up on the news, while there's no children hogging the television,' I turned on the six o'clock news. 'Isn't that tragic? Another terrible car crash.'

'The driver, believed to be a young woman, two women in the back seat, and two small children were fatally injured,' the announcer was saying. 'The front seat passenger, a young man, was taken to Portuncula Hospital with serious injuries. The accident happened about two miles from Kilrickle on the main Dublin to Galway Road.'

I looked across the room at Eamon. Was he thinking the same?

'Of course it's not them. Now sit down and eat your chips before they get cold.' He snapped. He didn't want to consider the implications.

Instead I ran out to the gate. A neighbour was walking up the road. 'Have you an evening paper?' I shouted.

'There's no paper today. Why? What's wrong?'

'Ah, nothing,' I ran back in to the house.

What to do? We had no phone. Our dinner congealed on the plates.

Five minutes later, Eamon's younger sister Marguerite walked straight in to the kitchen with Deirdre, our sister-in-law.

One look at their faces was enough.

It was true.

Angela, Carol, and Sonia had been killed instantly in a head-on crash with another car coming from Galway. The two little ones, who had been sleeping, also died on impact. At that fatal moment, Thomas had bent down to change a music tape. He suffered injuries to his face, feet and pelvis. He did not lose consciousness, and was able to tell them that his brother was waiting for them at a pre-arranged place.

Unaware, Stephen waited by the side of the road, near Headford. He had become anxious as time passed, so he telephoned Carol's partner Harry at work in Dublin. All he could tell him was that they had left early.

Instead of his family, a police car pulled up beside Stephen.

Thomas spent months in hospital, bravely enduring painful operations. He was, and is, a cheerful fellow, very idealistic. He went on to study Art in Cork, gained a Masters, and now teaches there.

Sonia's heartbroken father took her remains back to London.

Angela had often spoken of her fear of being buried alive. When the huge funeral was over, her ashes, and those of Carol, little Emily and Jude, were sprinkled in a peaceful grave beneath Balscadden Castle near Rush, overlooking green fields rolling down to the sea.

All her troubles over.

Rows and rows of securely tied grapes snake up the hill on both sides of the lane. The parched dust powders my toes and sandals as we walk side by side. The still-hot evening sun warms our tanned shoulders and back. A glowing feeling of well-being exudes from my fit, trim body. I think of the scrumptious meal we've just eaten. Freshly grilled tuna steaks, garden peas, tiny French potatoes, washed down with chilled white wine.

I spot a magnificent praying mantis clinging motionless to the wire fence. The crickets are beginning to tune up for their night's performance.

I sneak my hand into Eamon's. He smiles lazily at me, and squeezes my fingers.

We walk on.

TO CATCH A BUS

It seemed fairly straightforward at the time. We were on holidays in County Clare, and Cailín, our beautiful eighteen-year-old daughter, had visited us for the weekend. She had to be back in Dublin by Monday evening to start her first job as a waitress.

As it would be a bank holiday, we enquired about the bus timetable in the tourist office. This was in the town, two miles away from the old house we rented. We were informed there would be one bus only on Monday morning – leaving at seven o'clock.

Nuala had introduced us to the beauty of County Clare, and every summer we looked forward to its pleasures of music, set dancing, and the Atlantic Ocean.

Accustomed as we were to rising late, we borrowed an alarm clock. Naturally, nobody heard it. Awakening at 6.50 a.m., I shouted for Cailín frantically as I struggled in to my clothes. She catapulted out of her room, down the stairs, out to the car, unwashed, unkempt, and unawake.

We made it to the town in five minutes.

A deserted place. Still asleep. No bus, no queue, nobody.

I knocked at a pub-cum-shop-cum-house. An old gent peeped out.

'Do you know anything about the bus to Dublin?'

'Yerra, you'll have to ask the woman who owns the bus stop. It's outside her bakery down the road. She gets paid a few bob for allowing CIÉ put it outside her shop.

As we hurried away he added, 'You'd want to bang hard on her door. She's a bit on the deaf side. But if you do, it'll be the last time you'll knock, because she's fierce cranky!'

We knocked timidly. Then desperately. No answer.

I spied the lady next door as she popped out to take in her milk. Pulling her dressing gown tight, she called out, 'She's probably at Mass.'

Sure enough we heard church bells ringing. We raced around the corner to the church. Locked up. Not a sinner in sight.

We decided to try the hotel nearby. Surely someone must be up there. In the reception hall we encountered five elderly Americans, togged out in jogging gear. No sign of any staff though.

'Probably had to make their own breakfast,' Cailín whispered.

'Who told you there was a bus today, honey?' One of them enquired.

We explained.

'If I were you I'd go back to the tourist office and complain. But it's hardly worth your while – they are closed today – bank holiday, I believe.'

'What will you do if you don't find your bus?' A blue-rinsed lady asked.

'Go back to bed.'

So we did.

Next morning we tried again. The town was alive. Real people everywhere. Bravely we marched into the bakery shop – me bringing up the rear.

Cailín faced the tidy old woman.

'Is there a bus today please?'

'Of course there's a bus,' she barked, 'It leaves at nine o'clock sharp.'

'Is there just one bus?'

'Aren't you lucky to have a bus at all!' Impatiently, our cross informant marched off to her back parlour.

It was only half eight. We stood vigilantly on the spot outside the bakery. Nine o'clock came. No sign. Ten past. The call of nature necessitated Cailín to dash off. I stood guard. Around the corner advancing towards me, was the BUS!

The thought crossed my mind that maybe I should put out my hand. But this was the country, not Dublin. It would stop of course.

It didn't.

It whizzed past as I limply raised my hand. A breathless Cailín joined me. We watched its backside disappear in a cloud of fumes out the greeny road.

Cailín caught the bus back to Dublin on Wednesday. Her new employers told her she wasn't needed. I don't think they believed her explanation.

BRAVO

As Dad got older, he mellowed and softened. He loved writing about unknown corners of Ireland, and still retained an optimistic, childlike curiosity and enthusiasm for life.

He would set off on his latest assignment, immaculately attired in beige. Always in beige.

Shirt, trousers, linen jacket. Stout, tan-laced brogues – highly polished – army style. Donegal-tweed hat plonked firmly down to his ears. Bright eyes twinkling beneath his arched bushy eyebrows. There was a vibrancy, an aura of excitement about him as he embarked on each new discovery.

Now he was the respected *seanchaí* of journalism.

Doors opened for him wherever he turned up, and we reaped some of the benefits. In latter years, Dad gave our family the attention that his own younger children had been deprived of. He admired and respected Eamon as a hard-working family man. When Dad had a peculiar stroke, which left him 'walking slightly sideways', he elected Eamon as his guide, placing his trust and his hand on Eamon's shoulder.

Surprise treats included regular trips to the Zoo, strawberries from Wexford, racks of lamb via the exclusive Mirabeau restaurant. When Ireland's new Boeing 747 made its maiden flight from Dublin to Shannon, myself and five of his grandsons swept through the VIP lounge behind Dad, and were ushered aboard – a super experience for us all.

One pleasant summer's day, Dad organised a picnic to Ireland's Eye from Howth Harbour. About ten of us crammed into a long motor boat. Hugh platters of seafood and salads were handed down and we balanced them on our knees as we put-putted over to the Island. The seagulls were not happy about our arrival. They swirled above our heads, screeching loudly. It was not a very comfortable picnic!

When Irish Ferries launched their brand-new ferry to Holyhead – with invited press of course – Eamon, our older boys, some granddaughters, and Niamh were invited along also. Drink and food were complimentary, but an unexpected storm left most of the passengers vomiting, or lying on the newly carpeted floor.

'Your dad, Ciarán, and the captain were the only ones not sick. When dinner was served, there was an awful lot of empty chairs. Ciarán demolished two dinners!' Eamon told me that evening.

When we were in our late thirties, Eamon and I took to visiting Mam and Dad each Saturday night. It was our weekly treat – a break from our demanding throng.

Dad would prepare a gourmet meal for us – from his continental recipe book – worthy of a five-star hotel, a surprise menu each time. The table in the dining room, resplendent with a crisp linen cloth, finest delft, sparkling glassware, fresh flowers, and a basket each for the bottles of red and white vintage wines.

Accompanying these visual and yummy delights, Dad's choice of classical music became an integral part of the evening.

Music had always been an essential part of Dad's life. He tolerated Mam's choices of Frank Sinatra, Glenn Miller and old, popular standards, but classical music was his.

***

In the drab pre-television days of the fifties, when black winter evenings ensured we children stayed indoors, Dad invited song and music into our lives. In the cosy room he called the den, he taught us simple German and French tunes his sensitive ear had picked up on his travels. He was then working for the Irish Tourist Board.

I can see Nuala and Gráinne standing to attention in front of him singing 'Count Your Blessings One by One', Dad, de-da-ing along, vigorously conducting with waving hands. Without losing his rhythm, he would pounce on each in turn with a pointed finger – one to climb towards the high notes, the other to harmonise an octave below.

He constructed his own wireless, complete with cone-shaped speaker, which he placed on the top shelf of a bookcase. It was quite usual to see him standing in front of it, enraptured, as a classical symphony crackled and thundered throughout the house.

When I was seventeen, Dad offered me tickets to the prom in the Gaiety Theatre. I had no idea what a prom was – I had a vague notion of a concert, but I naively accepted.

Inappropriately dressed in Gráinne's borrowed cardigan and tight skirt, I cringed in my plush crimson seat on the balcony, stiff with embarrassment and boredom, as waves of unintelligible sounds reverberated around me. I felt alienated from the rows of black-tied, evening-suited, middle-aged faces. This confusion of noise and snobbery, connotations of elitism, was not for me.

But twenty years later, on those pleasant evenings, this music began to beguile me. Even though I did not know Bach from

Brahms, I would catch myself humming a bar or two as I hung out the washing on weekdays. I became impatient for Saturday and when we would arrive, Dad would enquire, 'Any requests?'

Awkwardly, I would whistle my desired choice.

'Ah yes. That's Mahler's *Adagio* – from his Fifth,' or, 'Sounds like Mozart's slow movement from his Symphony Number 21. Good girl!'

And so, gradually I became addicted. I began to recognise different composers and to appreciate their uplifting music.

On Christmas Day, 1979 (it was to be his last Christmas) Dad was, as usual, handing out beautifully wrapped presents to all the family. I was given a tiny envelope. Inside, on a Christmas card, he'd written 'it's too big – try the bedroom.'

There I found a square cardboard box that contained a brand-new stereogram.

And so, with my very own stereo installed in our sitting room, I purchased Beethoven's *Pastoral Symphony*. Even the children liked that. Gradually, availing of Dad's extensive record collection, it was mutually gratifying to share my discovery of a 'new' symphony by Sibelius or a moving concerto by Brahms.

As I go about my housework, I choose music to match my mood or occupation. If my nerves are frazzled, Brahms' Second Piano Concerto calms me down. Feeling energetic? Saint-Saëns' Organ Concerto blows the house apart. Haydn's *Surprise Symphony* is perfect for dispelling gloom. Rachmaninov's Piano Concerto is ideal for tidying upstairs – it lasts for nearly an hour. If I'm trying to get the children out of bed quickly, a blast of Richard Strauss's *Zarathustra* usually works! If they grumble about my music,

Barber's *Adagio* or Shostakovich's *Gadfly* soothes them into submission.

Now, late at night, when they are all fast asleep upstairs, and quietness folds upon our home, I listen to Lyric FM, or choose a CD of my own. As the anguish of maybe a Wagner aria, or perhaps the beauty of Richard Strauss's *Alpine Symphony*, tugs and twists my heart with joyful pain, I think of Dad and the priceless gift he bequeathed to me.

How strange… I barely noticed as he gave it.

THE VISITOR

There were plenty of soft drinks, wine and spirits in Dad's locker.

'Eamon, could you get us some Guinness?'

Always the host, Dad was propped up in bed wearing fresh pyjamas. His bleak hospital room was clean and neat. Plants ranged along the narrow window ledge. All in readiness.

I waited by the window. At exactly five minutes to three, far down below in the VIP car park, two long black limos pulled up. Two grey-suited men emerged from the first car.

Special branch.

In no time they had checked the wards on the fourth floor. Staff nurse had been instructed to allow no one access while he was there. Inspection over, they took up positions, one on either side of the door to Dad's private room.

At three o'clock he breezed in the door, hand outstretched to

Dad, a big smile on his florid face. Compared to Dad's ghostly whiteness, he exuded health and energy. As he pulled a chair close to the bed, he introduced the man accompanying him as his Public Relations Officer. 'That could have been you, Terry. But you turned me down!' he laughed.

In the early days, before he became Taoiseach, he had offered Dad the job.

Mam and I were introduced. He wasn't interested in us though. 'You know Charlie, I've a sixty-forty chance of beating this leukaemia.'

'Never mind the odds. As soon as you're well enough, we'll fly you down in my helicopter to Inishvickillane to recuperate.'

Dad leaned towards Charlie and whispered something. Discreetly the bedpan was slid under the covers.

A kerfuffle outside the door turned out to be Eamon trying to gain admittance as his brown paper bag was scrutinised by the special branch men.

Refreshments were refused.

'I gave up drinking and smoking years ago,' the Taoiseach informed us. 'When you see a photo of me in the papers, holding a wine glass, that's spring water I'm drinking.'

He and Dad chatted about old times, exchanging stories, forgetting about us.

At five minutes to five, Charlie stood up in symmetry with his right hand man. At exactly the same time, the door was opened wide.

Dad was very tired.

Shaking hands with each of us, the dapper little man departed swiftly, his shiny blue suit flashing through the empty corridor. He was top of the heap: Taoiseach of our country with a mansion in Kinsealy and an island retreat – wealth and health.

He needed nothing from Dad, had nothing to gain. They both knew Dad was dying. He was never going to write another column for his newspaper.

Just two old Joey's pupils. Friends.

REQUIEM

Although in his late sixties, Dad continued to travel and work until two months before he died. He had told no one that he had been fighting leukaemia secretly for over two years.

One calm afternoon in late September, his energy ran out. Having slowly dressed for work, his weary hands refused to knot his tie. He sat thoughtfully a while on the stool beside the phone, little finger hooked between his teeth, head tilted sideways, as though listening. His driver, Tom, waited outside the flat to drive Dad to his various appointments.

Tom drove him to the hospital instead.

Next day, the doctors told us of the seriousness of his illness. I visited myself that same evening. 'Cheer up, daughter,' he commanded. 'My doctor says I've a sixty-forty chance of beating this with chemotherapy.' He raised his skinny arm in the air, and made a firm fist. 'No surrender!' A crooked grin lit up his thin face.

And so began two months of horrifying, sickening treatment. He battled on bravely, his emaciated body growing weaker. But never his spirit.

'Only four more (three more, two more, one more) weeks!' He'd declare optimistically, punching the stale hospital air.

His private room was akin to a hospitality suite. Flowers, plants, wine in his locker. Every visitor was offered a chair, a drink. Dad's cheerful voice entertained them with anecdotes from the bed – the hateful drip ignored.

The awful wait for D-Day ended.

We waited for Dad's doctor to reveal whether the chemo had worked or not. At three o'clock he arrived on the fifth floor. He then proceeded on a leisurely tour through the wards at the far end of the corridor. Isolated inside Dad's room, we chattered desperately in whispers while we waited, petering into silence when we heard brisk footsteps approaching. There was a slight pause in his gait as he drew level outside Dad's door, then a quickening as he hurried on to the end of the corridor, then clattered down the stairs.

My father's tired grey-blue eyes opened wide and caught mother's brimming eyes in his. He stretched out his hand to her. Neither spoke.

Some time later my dad chuckled wistfully and, turning his face to the wall, embraced the awaiting coma.

He died one week later, on 5 December 1980.

During that week when he was unconscious, Niamh and I brought a tape recorder up to his room. We played some of his favourite music: Borodin, Schubert, and Saint-Saëns' Piano Concerto – a lively piece.

Just like him.

DO YOU WANT TO BE FAMOUS?

Ever wondered how it would feel to be famous?

To be stopped on the street because your face was recognised? To be mobbed? To be asked the same question over and over again? I can tell you from personal experience that it is not that exciting or wonderful.

You see – I was famous once. Well, twice actually.

The first occasion. I won a competition especially for housewives, and the illustrious title of 'Mrs Shopping Centre'. Suffice to explain that if it were today, 'Mrs Nutgrove' or 'Mrs Artane Castle' would be similar.

To qualify one had to be alive, female, reasonably articulate, and a frequent shopper. At the press reception in the Shelbourne Hotel, I gasped with delight and surprise as my name was announced as the winner. It had been tough beating the other finalists – an eight months' pregnant mammy, a granny, and three other shoppers who lived further from the shopping centre than me. Amidst popping champagne and flashing cameras, I was adorned with a sash and presented with a cheque for one hundred and fifty pounds.

Escorted through the congratulatory crowds to a quiet annexe, I was interviewed by the press. I was asked penetrating questions such as 'How often do you shop?' and 'What are you going to do with your prize money?' (I bought the ladies in our cul-de-sac a necklace each and took the family out to a candle-lit dinner – even hiring a coach to drive us there and back!)

Next day my photograph was in all the papers. One imaginative and flattering caption above my picture read – 'A proper shopper'. Everywhere I went I was congratulated. I was a mini-celebrity, at least in my part of Dublin. And I'd done nothing!

During my year's reign, I mixed with and met fellow professionals. I nearly danced with Mike Murphy. He and I were the stars of a special promotion. On one occasion I was mobbed. Honestly!

My important assignment for that day was to appear glamorous, don my sash, stroll through the shopping centre and distribute free tights to the public. I set off through the arcade, smiling and pleasantly exchanging a few words with the first ladies I met, rather like the Queen might.

However, as word spread through the shops, within a few minutes I was surrounded by scores of shouting women.

'Give us a pair of tights missus!'

'Don't mind that aul one – she got two already!'

Two bouncers had to rescue me from the centre of flailing hands and flying nylons – red-faced and dishevelled. All in the line of duty, of course.

But it was great fun, being Mrs Somebody. I was treated royally by everyone connected with the competition. I handed over my sash in the Gresham Hotel the following year to another dazed housewife, and settled back into familiar anonymity.

Until 1988.

As a member of the audience in the *Late Late Show* – momentarily lulled by the downlighting and cosy atmosphere of the studio into believing that it was just Gay, his guest and us having this nice little chat – I happened to articulate an opinion. I forgot that three-quarters of the population of Ireland were watching.

Next morning on the way to the shops, I was stopped five times. 'Saw you on the telly last night.'

The pattern was set for the weekend. *The Late Late* was the only topic. Apart from my neighbours, children and relatives, the check-out girl in Dunnes and three ladies at the church door, even my local chemist stopped business for a few minutes whilst customers and staff discussed the show.

By Monday, I cycled to my English class with relief, only to be greeted by a round of applause when I walked in. My teacher, Síle, apologised for not seeing the show. At coffee break strangers approached me. Buying some meat on the way home, the butcher smiled as he handed me my change. 'Saw you on the *Late Late* on Saturday.'

I no longer knew what to say.

'Thank you. Did you? It was nothing… I was only a member of the audience, not the bloomin' guest!'

Tuesday – I stayed home – hibernating until Friday's show. Somebody else's turn. I really felt sorry for the man who sang hello to his folks back home. Probably famous for at least a week, while I merged gratefully back into the ranks of the unknown.

I don't think I'd be able for fame a third time!

I hear the rustle of the post being shoved through the letterbox, then the muffled plop as it hits the hall floor. Holding my breath, I hurry out quickly and bend to pick it up. The letter is there. My results. My hands shake slightly as I carefully open the envelope.

I enjoyed sitting the English Leaving Cert exam after thirty-five years away from school. It was a little embarrassing that the principal thought I was a supervisor when I arrived at her school. The teenagers in the classroom, doing the same exam as me, became quite giggly when I sat down, and whispered to each other after I had asked for more paper. My selfless teacher, Síle, and the family expected me to do well.

Is that an A? Where are my glasses? Yes, it is an A.

Joy is me.

SLEEP

Christmas night of 1984, Mrs Brady was very tired, but the noise of her sons, daughters, and grandchildren having a singsong down in the kitchen didn't dint her good humour.

Back at work for the January sales, she kept an eye out for a Communion dress for our little Clare. I went into town and bought the one Mrs Brady had picked out, but oddly, she wasn't there. She had not been feeling well and had taken a rare day off.

Pauline, the youngest daughter, had moved back to Bradys' with her three young sons. Despite her protests, Pauline got the doctor for her mam. As she sat in her chair by the fire, she insisted that she was just tired. He said she needed rest, her chest didn't sound too good, and he'd come back the following day.

That night, as usual, Mrs Brady retired to her double bed, with her little grandson, Anthony.

Some time later Pauline heard Mrs Brady's faithful dog, Prince, who followed her everywhere – even into the confession box once – barking in the hall. She went to investigate. The dog was standing taut and bristling, staring fixedly up the stairs.

When Pauline went up to check on her mother she saw that she was dead – the sleeping boy beside her. She had been very tired indeed. Her worn-out heart just stopped beating.

I lost my second mother – more real to me than my poor dear mother sitting alone in her flat in Clontarf.

IS IT ABOUT A BIKE?

In October 1958, I was sweet sixteen. I purchased a brand-new bike on the never-never. I paid thirty shillings deposit, then cycled it home. Every Saturday after that I paid two shillings and sixpence off it to McHugh's shop on the North Strand. I reckoned I'd own it by the time I was eighteen.

It was blue, a racer with drop handlebars, and the latest fashion.

I cycled to work in town along the sea wall at Dollymount each morning. Happily, I let the number 30 bus pass me by, thinking of all the money I'd save on bus fares.

As time passed and the mornings grew colder, I began to wish I was sitting, warm and cosy, on the comfy bus, when its slipstream enveloped me as it whizzed past. The sea wind always seemed to be against me. My hands were icy, my neck stiff, and my back ached from bending over the handlebars.

In the office where I worked in O'Connell Street, we dealt with the public. We were expected to look smart and were not allowed to wear slacks. I invariably arrived late – lacquered hair standing to attention, complete with blue face, red nose, and runny eyes.

Sweat trickled down the back of my nylon blouse, while the seams of my nylons meandered crazily down my cold legs.

One dark January evening I emerged from the office, tying a chiffon scarf under my chin, ready for the dreaded journey back home. I looked at the spot where my bike should be. It was not there. Vanished. Stolen. A rare happening in those days. It had never occurred to me to purchase a lock.

I couldn't believe my luck. Now I'd have to travel to work on the bus. Great!

Bee-hived beautifully, sickly white-pink lipstick in tact, black eyeliner perfect, elegant straight seams. And luxury – I could wear my skin-tight black straight skirt!

Of course I had to pay off all the two and sixpences until I owned the bike I no longer possessed, but it was worth it. No more bikes for me.

But, thirty years later…

Driving home one night, Eamon and I spied a crock of a bicycle left outside on the path for the annual householders' junk collection. 'I could make you a grand bike with the wheels from that and the bits we have lying in our shed,' he suggested.

So we pinched it. And he did. A mongrel of a bike, complete with a back carrier. I painted the finished machine with black shiny paint, and my 'black bomber' was born!

Now we're inseparable. It sits happily outside the supermarket, library, or church, *sans* lock. Waiting just for me alone.

It's rusty and battered now. No self-respecting thief would be bothered robbing it. Not even the children will borrow it. But to me it spells freedom, fitness and speed. I like the wind in my hair, and streaming eyes don't bother me.

Wasn't it kind of the years to have dimmed my vanity?

AUNT KIT

Each year, during the long summers when we were children, Mam sent one or two of us down to our Grandaunt Kit in Athlone.

As a young woman, Kit had come up from Kerry to work in the Athlone picture house, playing the piano to accompany the silent films. She had met and married a much older man, Jim Egan, and moved into his grocery-cum-pub. They had no children of their own, and we were treated with kindness.

Kit was a tall, angular woman, with a thin high-boned face, and startlingly watery blue eyes.

Constantly on the go, she had an abundance of wild, wavy grey hair precariously plaited on top of her head, stray wisps falling about her face. A flowered greasy apron, tied tightly at the front, was part of her daily attire.

Jim was mild-mannered to her lively wiriness, and she managed their business with a slapdash briskness. On market day, the front room was turned into a dining room, and Kit cooked massive dinners for the visiting traders.

We were expected to help. The dinners were cooked down in the steamy, messy kitchen.

I would carry the heavy plates piled with bacon and cabbage and spuds to the customers, or fetch them a bottle of stout from behind the wooden counter of the shop.

I loved serving: scooping up sugar from the huge sack on the flag-stoned floor, measuring it carefully into brown paper bags on the scales whilst balancing the copper weights on the opposite side. On busy days, Kit rewarded me with a bottle of cordial, and a handful of broken biscuits from the glass-fronted tin boxes. I would slip into the 'snug', burrow into the faded velvet of the once - plush seats, close the door, and pretend that this was my little house.

They kept pigs and hens out the back in a long, narrow concreted yard. I was feeding the pigs one morning, and took off my new apple-green cardigan. I hung it on the low fence bordering their sty. I turned to watch Jim chase a hen around the yard. He caught it by the neck, then in one swift movement, flashed the hatchet and chopped off its head. Turning away, I spied the pigs slurping up the swill, bits of my green cardigan mashed through the smelly mess.

Years later, My younger brother Don recounted the following story.

Dad had sent him down to Kit. (On his bike! My sisters and I always went by train.) He was thirteen years old, and had never been to Athlone before. He slept in a ditch in the Midlands that night, and arrived at the Egans' door next morning, wet, hungry, and weary. They fed him, bought him new clothes, and put him in charge of a particular piglet.

'My little piggie took to me, because if it didn't like you, you were in deep "trouble",' he remembered.

As summer went on, his pig got bigger and bigger and he decided to give it a treat: take it out of its sty, tether it to a fence, and concrete its mucky home. Don's first cement mix. Not too bad, just a little too fluid. Another day on the fence for the pig. Next morning, satisfied with its quarters, Don allowed the fellow back to its newly floored home.

The pig proceeded to eat the moist grey mess. All of it. Every scrap of it.

When the pig was about eight foot long and weighed a quarter of a ton, Jim took it to market, and sold it.

'Although I cried at the loss of my friend, my tears dissolved into helpless laughter at the thought of concrete rashers!' Don chuckled.

As for me, Uncle Jim would bring me out to his patch of bog on the bar of his bicycle. Underneath the vast cloudy sky, and miles of flat bare land, I would sit on his folded jacket and watch as he sliced clean, wet cuts of turf, then piled the fresh sods into a tent-like shape. They reminded me of giant slices of moist Christmas pudding.

My job was to mind our lunch.

Jim didn't chat at all, but his was a kindly presence. At midday, he'd sit down beside me, hand me a bottle of lemonade and some fig rolls for my picnic, while he munched on sandwiches, washed down with a bottle of stout.

Every Saturday, Kit gave us four pence each for the matinee in the cinema. It was on the far side of the bridge over the Shannon. There was always a long queue. One rainy afternoon, as I peeped through the gaps in the bridge at the dark murky water below, my hands slipped on the smooth surface, and my precious money dropped down into the hostile river.

I ran all the way back to Connaught Street, heartbroken and tearful. Kit comforted me, hugging my head against her bony chest. I could smell the dinners, the grease, the beer, all the hard work, as my nose pressed into her worn apron.

***

Jim died some years later. Kit soldiered on in the dank and dirty home, the business long gone, the window of the shop unchanged, mottled Sweet Afton cigarette cut-outs, dried dead flies and dusty stout bottles.

Her kind neighbour found her one cold January morning, suffering from hypothermia, and had her hospitalised. When Kit was well enough to be discharged, we found a comfortable nursing home for her, and I accompanied her to her new abode. The nurses had informed her of the decision. Kit sat bowed, clean and neat, in a wheelchair.

Waiting.

'I want to go back home, Deirdre,' her pale face turned up to me. I feigned a casual cheerfulness.

'You can't go back Kit. You need to be looked after. You'll like the nursing home. It's cosy. And the nurse is from Kerry – just like you.'

But that spring afternoon, as I waved goodbye to my aunt, shrunken in an armchair by the fire – her ancient black handbag clutched in her thin brittle fingers – I knew that her spirit was broken.

***

When she died, my sister Gráinne and I were the chief mourners. Nuala had travelled down with us, but she was unwell, and returned to Dublin on the train. We were ushered into the front parlour by the cheery nurse. A mahogany table took up most of the space. On it rested the coffin. The blind had been pulled down, but in the gloom I could make out the profile of my aged aunt.

Sharp thin nose, tightly pursed lips, soft silver hair brushed neatly to one side, clasped in a brown slide. As I stood there, I remembered a framed photo of Kit as a young woman. Perfect, delicate face, shining eyes, and masses of long wavy tresses.

After the funeral, the nursing home served up a lavish dinner and drinks for the few mourners who'd turned up. Good neighbours, vague relatives. When the meal was over, Gráinne stood up in front of the fireplace, cleared her throat loudly, and announced, 'Ladies and gentlemen, my sister and I have to head back to Dublin shortly. I, as executrix of my aunt's will, am going to read it out now.'

Like a scene from a James Joyce story.

Instantly there was an expectant hush.

As Gráinne read on there was the odd laugh, 'You won't be buying that new car now John', or 'hard luck', as distant cousins were passed over.

My heart jumped with pleasure when I heard my own name called out. Kit had left me two thousand pounds!

As we said our goodbyes, I was congratulated good-naturedly by all.

I was so grateful. 'Isn't that wonderful? So thoughtful of dear Kit. And weren't the nurses kind to give us such a spread?' I said to Gráinne, as we bounced our way back to Dublin in Gráinne's bumpy mini.

'Don't be fooled Di. The bill for all that drink and food will be sent to me.'

***

170

I had promised Mammy I'd call and tell her how everything went. She was in bed, reading. She had not been up to going herself. Kit was her aunt. She half-listened to me – glancing down now and then at the open page of her book.

'…and Kit left you money too,' I finished quietly.

'How much?'

'Two thousand pounds!'

'Is that all?' She bent her head and continued reading her book.

A DAMAGED WOMAN

'I've a clean bill of health from the waist up.' Mam tightened the belt of her smart raincoat as she walked down the steps of the hospital to our car. Two weeks without alcohol or cigarettes had done her good. Clear-eyed, bright-skinned, thick wavy hair, glowing with health.

'Eamon dear, will you stop at the off-licence on the way? I want to buy coke for Máiréad and Clare and a Guinness for yourself and Di. And you can get me a bottle of Sandyman's Port.'

I leaned forward from the back seat.

'Mam. You know you're not supposed to drink.'

'Oh my doctor said it would do me good to have the odd glass of port.'

She fibbed charmingly. So happy to be 'sprung' again.

***

Mam was docile and subdued whenever she had to be institutionalised, accepting the routine, burying herself in her books. Yet as soon as she was back home, her sad, solitary life resumed. Bed for days on end, sustained by warm milk with pepper, gruel, biscuits, or a dinner left for her, while she read and read.

Or, brushed and lipsticked, her heavy square basket tucked in the crook of her arm, she'd walk the familiar route to her local. There she would ensconce herself in a corner, glasses halfway down her nose, to read her book and drink double gins, until one of her kind friends would drive her home and link her into her flat.

This was Mam's life after Dad. She was lost without him. He had been her only love.

She had got through his funeral and the Christmas after he died in a haze of tablets and alcohol. Then it really hit her. He was gone. One Thursday evening in January, I called to find her sitting – quiet and still – hunched over in the armchair, fully dressed. She was sober. Wringing her soft hands painfully together, she lifted her poor grief-ravaged face and looked up at me with tear-worn eyes. 'Oh, Deirdre… I miss him so much…so much.'

I could only put my arms around her.

***

Gráinne dropped in regularly, and Nuala, who now lived in Dublin, took Mam out in her car. Our gang visited every Sunday.

Niamh put on Mam's favourite records, the little ones bopped around, and Mam danced with Eamon. 'What wonderful rhythm you have,' she'd declare breathlessly as she sank back into her armchair in front of the electric fireplace. Moderately inebriated, briefly happy, her gaze fixed wistfully on the past, she told us of wonderful times 'with your father'. She said that 'inside this old body there's still an eighteen-year-old girl.'

Back in the present, she could be artfully tactless. When Cailín, our first daughter was born, Mam's comment was 'Congratulations, Deirdre. Pity she's so plain!' And to seventeen-year-old Ciarán, 'Why don't you shave off that dreadful moustache?'

It was a waste of time phoning Mam, as she was apt to put the phone down abruptly.

She expressed little interest in the lives of her scattered children. She was sweet and polite when they visited her, but didn't bother to hide the fact that she had certain favourites. She had scribbled a poem once on a page torn from a novel, which began 'I am a damaged woman...'

***

That Sunday after we collected her from the hospital, back in her sitting room, we put on Gilbert O'Sullivan's tape and danced to 'Matrimony'. Mam sang 'Alone Again, Catherine' to the line 'Alone Again, Naturally'. Her next request was for 'Hello' by Lionel Ritchie. Mam had heard it when she was in hospital. 'It reminds me so much of your father. I expect him to walk in the door any minute.'

She was so sad.

I watched her neck and face flush redder as she drank the bottle of port.

***

On Tuesday, Eamon and I called to bring Mam to the library as usual. She got her nine books in Howth – she had all our tickets as well as her own – and afterwards she insisted on buying us a pint. She gulped down her little glass of port, then tapped the table impatiently, waiting for us. As we drove her home, she was unusually quiet.

'It hasn't got the same kick as gin,' she murmured as we left her at her door.

The following Sunday we arrived in a flurry at her flat. It was a glorious September afternoon. Máiréad and Clare played as we waited outside the door. I held a side plate of Eamon's home-cooked dinner in one hand, some roses from our garden in the other.

No answer.

'It's through the kitchen window again.' I looked meaningfully at Eamon.

***

So many times Mammy had been found in a heap on the floor of her bedroom. Too many sleeping tablets, or gin, or both. We – Nuala, Gráinne and I, her eldest children – had tried to confront her about the damage to herself.

We'd called one day, and it was decided that I should voice our worries. I knocked and went into her bedroom.

'What are you all doing here?' she demanded suspiciously.

'Mam, we're all worried about you. You've got to start taking care. You can't go on like this. You'll be found dead someday if you keep this up. If you go on neglecting yourself, we'll be forced to do something…'

I stood at the foot of her bed, hurting, and helpless. I could feel her anger across the room.

She raised herself up, leaned forward toward me, and hissed, 'How dare you! How dare you! It's none of your business. Your father left me enough money to live the way I choose. You take care of your own family. You're NOT going to send me anywhere. I'll die in my own home. Now...GET OUT!'

***

Eamon lifted seven-year-old Máiréad up to the opened window. I watched her soft roundy legs disappear in a flounce of tartan, and a minute later she opened the front door wide for us, with an important grin on her heart-shaped face.

The gloomy bedroom was empty. There was no note in the kitchen. Mam usually left a message if she had gone down to the pub. She knew we always called. I was angry.

'We'll just leave everything. I'm not waiting around.'

Máiréad tugged my hand. 'I have to go to the toilet.'

So we waited for her.

'I can't open the door. There's something in my way,' I heard her call out.

I stood where I was. Eamon ran to the bathroom.

'Ring for an ambulance quick,' he shouted.

I cuddled my two small girls tightly as I watched them carry out my mother's body on a stretcher. She looked really well, I thought, Her hair newly dressed, face flushed a deep pink, only her soft hands were a ghostly white colour. Still wearing her wine velvet dressing gown.

175

She had been preparing herself for our visit. An empty bottle of gin was found under her.

Who would have thought she would die suddenly from a massive heart attack? In her own bathroom.

She got her wish.

The familiar signature tune of the Late Late Show. *Tense and waiting. What time is she coming on? Gay, the smooth professional, will probably save her for the last item. He does.*

It's obvious that Nuala is very nervous. I can't see her hands, but I bet they are clenched together. Gay is kind, but his questions probe gently. She answers him in quiet bursts of shocking honesty. There are tears in her eyes as she talks about the family – her memories, her life, her feelings.

Her truth.

Nuala skips the after show get-together, and drives straight home to Ranelagh. She is alone, still shaking, when I ring her.

'I thought you were very brave and sincere.'

'Thanks Di – you're the only one who telephoned.'

WEAR AND TEAR

'You need to have a hysterectomy. How soon can you come in? Next Thursday suit you?'

The doctor's matter-of-fact tone, as though he were commenting on the pleasant weather, extracted a shaky 'OK' from me. It was a shiny new February morning, and my fortieth birthday. I had come to see this specialist because of persistent anaemia, which had been draining me for years.

It was my addiction to raw cabbage that finally forced me to see my GP. My jaws ached from munching mouthfuls of it throughout the day. He quickly diagnosed severe iron deficiency, caused by heavy periods. He put me on a course of iron tablets, then injections, but my blood count still kept plummeting. The possibility of a hysterectomy had been mentioned, so I shouldn't have been surprised by the specialist's decision.

But that lovely spring morning, I felt scared.

A motherly nurse handed me an admittance card. Like an obedient child I mumbled 'thanks', stuffing it in to my handbag. I hurried down the long, narrow, vinyl-covered corridor, pushed open the huge heavy doors, clattered down the steps, then stood still.

I stared up at the curtained windows of the wards above. I would be up there next week. How would I feel? What would the operation consist of? How would my family cope without me? I felt small, vulnerable, alone and trapped.

When I told the family, they were naturally sympathetic and supportive, but they were as ignorant of what a hysterectomy involved as I was. It did not console me when well-meaning friends said, 'Sure that's a common operation nowadays. You'll be grand!' The night before I was due to be admitted, I decided I was not going to go through with it.

Next morning I presented myself at outpatients, and waited nervously to explain to the doctor that I wasn't ready. When the nurse said at last, 'You can go in now,' all I could manage to say to the doctor was 'I can't…'

His eyes twinkled kindly behind gold-framed glasses. He patted my head.

'That's all right, dear. It's your womb, your decision. Take the time you need and then come back and see me.'

My gratitude was wordless. I had gained a reprieve. I settled back into safe domesticity. But after a few months I knew I had no choice. I needed the operation. So I determined to find out all I could to take away the gnawing fear.

The hospital had given me a leaflet with a few brief details. Small comfort. I discovered a marvellous book in the library, written by a counsellor who had had a hysterectomy herself. All my worries were dealt with in detail: femininity, sexuality, physical and emotional problems. The various types of hysterectomies were explained, and what to expect afterwards.

On a wild September afternoon, with a more positive frame of mind, I was admitted. The nurses were welcoming, kind, and cheerful. They explained each test and procedure. I was encouraged to chat with patients who were few days over their operation. The 'gyny' ward had sixteen beds. There was one private room for very ill patients, rather than the wealthy. The fact that I was a public patient did not make the slightest difference to the caring treatment I received.

Next morning, after a shower and a dozy pre-med tablet, I was wheeled to the operating theatre. In a hazy, sad sort of way, I said goodbye to my worn-out little womb that had carried seven babies. I felt warm tears trickle into my ears. My doctor's face peered down at me, smiling. Then all was blissfully black.

Regaining consciousness that evening, I was woozy and thirsty. During the night I was given painkilling injections, and next morning I had a refreshing bed bath. I was in the first bed nearest the nurses' station. On day two I had a wobbly walk, and was promoted to the second bed.

The third day I burst into tears because I couldn't eat my jelly and ice-cream. A kindly nurse put her arm around me, and explained that this was post-operative blues and would pass. It did, and my appetite improved. Eventually I ended up in number eight bed at the end of the ward, with my own sunny window.

Every day a physiotherapist came into our ward to do gentle exercises with all the post-op patients. I made friends with other women from all streams of life. I met a delicate midwifery teacher from Wales, who looked like a young Audrey Hepburn. She floated around in a silk dressing gown, quietly concentrating on her tummy exercises. She wanted to be back at work in six weeks. A life-torn ageing traveller woman, with waist-length white hair, used to sit in the chair beside her bed all day long. She never had any visitors, and addressed everyone as 'Ma'am'.

All of us jumbled together. Sad to think we would probably never see each other again.

Ten days later I was ready to go home. My doctor, immaculately dressed in tweeds of the same hue as his neat silvery hair, breezed over to my bed.

'If you were an oldish car, let's say I've completely reconditioned you. You're good for another 50,000 miles at least,' he declared.

Not very flattering perhaps, but encouraging. I'd had a bladder repair as well.

The toughest time of all was when I got home.

Nothing had prepared me for this. I got out of the car, walked three paces to the gate, and was exhausted. By the time I reached the dining-room sofa, I crumpled like a sack of potatoes. This terrible weariness persisted for about two weeks. But then, a gorgeous burst of energy promised a glimpse of what was to be my new self.

At first, I couldn't even lift the kettle, and used lie on the sofa, gazing at the balls of fluff on the carpet, not having the strength to vacuum or sweep. Kind neighbours looked after me when the family were out, and my sister-in-law, Deirdre, came every morning for two weeks and did all the heavy housework.

I was lucky, I had no depression. I'm sure I would have experienced the blues if I had not taken a positive approach to the operation.

I feel as much a woman as I did before, but fitter and healthier. I have a whole new zest for life.

There's a lot to be said for a properly reconditioned, oldish car, after all!

BRIEF ENCOUNTER

A dull, chilly day in Dublin City.

I'd just bought a pipe in Petersons, and was waiting to cross the road opposite Trinity College. Two elderly ladies stood beside me on the traffic island. Suddenly, the blank grey air was filled with the noise of police sirens.

At a furious speed, two garda motorcycles approached us from the top of Dame Street, followed by a long black limo.

Isolated and curious, I peered at the blackened windows, as the huge sleek car slowed almost to a stop in front of me at the sharp corner leading up to Grafton Street.

Silently, slowly, the back window wound down, and there, sitting less than two feet away, was none other than Nelson Mandela.

I gasped with recognition and delight, and just as I did so, he leaned towards me, and flashed the most beautiful, whitest, wonderful smile. At me. Me alone.

Instantly, the window slid shut and the limo sped off with a whoosh. The pedestrian lights turned green, but I stood still, dazed, as the two little women hurried on across the road.

'Did you see that?' I called after them. 'That was Nelson Mandela! He smiled at me. He must have been coming from Dublin Castle.'

One of them turned her head back and nodded, embarrassed.

I was lit up in a blaze of joy. My whole day had changed. I floated home on the bus, raced in the front door, dropped the shopping on the floor, and told the whole family about my moment.

After tea, Eamon went in to the front room to watch the six o'clock news.

'Deirdre,' he called. 'Your friend is on first.'

And there was Nelson – shaking hands, making speeches, waving farewell to Ireland.

My pal.

A LITTLE LEARNING

When a gap became available from my job as home-maker, I started to learn the piano again. Every Saturday, throughout a bitter winter, I went for my lesson to an eccentric old lady, Miss Boles, who lived on Clonliffe Road. A small, absent-minded, jolly woman, who looked rather like a comfy armchair. She had taught Eamon when he was a boy.

Musically she was a genius – she played the organ in Clonliffe College, and could play any stringed instrument brilliantly. She encouraged me to learn classical guitar as well, even though she explained that the ideal age to start was about six years old. I was thirty-eight.

Miss Boles lived in a dark redbrick house with her sister. Both were spinsters, even though Miss Boles had been engaged for over thirty years. Her gentleman friend would call for chats. He always wore a beret. I never saw her sister, but she did all the cooking, and I would hear her voice calling to say the dinner was ready.

Miss Boles' cat and her dog were the loves of her life. As I practised the scales, the animals munched their separate lunch bowls on the floor at my feet, blocking the heat from the electric fire. Seated on a chair beside me, Miss Boles balanced a large plate on her lap, instructing me to 'play that again' as she ploughed through her dinner.

Coming up to Christmas time, she showed me the presents she had bought for her pets – toy bones, jingly collars – 'But I'm hiding them until Christmas morning.'

Eamon bought a piano, and I drove the children berserk as I practised my pieces slowly and painfully.

I stopped going to lessons when our last baby arrived.

By the time Clare was ten and attending school independently, I decided to go back to learning. Coláiste Dhúlaigh had introduced the new concept of adult education, so I started off with Leaving Cert English.

We had an exceptional teacher, Síle Fitzgerald, who had obtained her teaching degree as a mature student herself. With a zest for life, Síle was a wonderfully giving teacher. She made us – a nervous, insecure bunch of oldish students – believe that anything was possible. She introduced us to the theatre – arranged tickets for *The Plough and the Stars*, *King Lear*, and other enjoyable productions. When our stimulating year was over, Síle threw a huge party in her house for us all – even organising us to perform a motley excerpt from *A Midsummer Night's Dream*.

Having sat one subject per year, I decided to give Art a try next, beginning with a night class, then a year in Kilbarrack, with a talented young artist called Sean.

We had to use a biro to draw. 'If I let you use pencils, you'll spend all your time rubbing out your mistakes,' our young teacher explained. He placed a chair on the table.

'Now I want you all to look at the spaces between, and draw the spaces only. Not the chair.' He made us draw the veins in a leaf, the lines in our hand. A gifted teacher.

After that class everything changed for me. It was as though I had been looking at the world with one eye. Now I could see the different shapes of the clouds, the shadows in a tree, the light glinting on the grass, shades and hues of colour.

After that I pursued drawing and painting, finishing up in the College of Art and Design.

I started off in a wreck of a room – cracked windows, high ceilings – at the top of Rutland Street School. Our class, mature ladies, unemployed young men, visiting students, visitors from abroad, had been hand-picked to do a foundation course for one year. Complete strangers that first day.

Awkward and shy, we were seated in a circle, drawing boards tilted, pencils at the ready.

'If you have come here to churn out "pretty pictures" for your family and friends, you're in the wrong place,' our lecturer Robert boomed. We turned to one and other, muttering things like 'of course not', 'last thing I want to do', and 'only children draw pretty pictures'.

How did he know that was just what I had in mind?

A young, handsome man, dressed in jeans and a T-shirt, entered our room without knocking.

'This is Brian. He is your life-drawing model. I'm giving you

185

twenty minutes to draw him, then I want you to pin your pictures on the wall with your name underneath. These will remind you of how bad you were in the weeks to come.' With that Robert left the room.

Brian hopped over a desk to the centre of the circle, took off all his clothes, then stood up on a wooden block, and assumed a pose.

A hush descended on the class. Heads bent down over drawing boards. Only the sound of charcoal busily rubbing on paper could be heard. The odd cough.

The students opposite me were safe – his bottom was facing them, but five of us had the distinction of attempting to draw a full-frontal nude. I concentrated seriously on the angular face, the dimple in the chin, the strong shoulders, the slim waist – working my way down. I sneaked a look at Sylvia's picture – she sat next to me. She had solved the problem by blacking in an area from the waist to the thighs. The old lady on my other side had drawn a huge torso with a tiny little thing. I suppressed a hysterical urge to giggle. With a deep breath I shaded in a suggestion of male appendage, hurriedly continuing on down the legs. The room was quite chilly, and I observed that the feet were a bluish tone as I finished.

I pinned the resulting portrait in a dark corner before Robert returned.

As the weeks passed, we lost our self-consciousness and looked forward to drawing nude male and female figures.

Just like drawing a chair.

The following year we moved to the Project Centre in City Quay, finishing up with an exhibition of our clothes – hanging on a line outside – constructed from wire and plaster of Paris. Mine was my jacket.

For my last year, inside the spooky surroundings of a once handsome convent in Portland Row, I brought home a beautiful sculpture of my arm and hand, and Eamon stuck it among the flowers in the back garden.

THANK YOU FOR THE DAYS

'Di? This is your long lost brother in London. I've an offer of a lift over on the ferry in me mate Frank's van. Can you put me up?'

Don's deep voice shouted over the phone.

'Sure, Don. When are you coming?'

'Hold on. Frank's here with me.'

I heard him address his friend.

'Frank, when are you sailing over to the auld sod?'

Then the phone went dead.

'Typical!' I muttered out loud.

'Typical what?'

Eamon was relaxing in front of the fire. I slumped on the sofa beside him and filled him in.

'Listen, Di. I like your charming, witty brother, always had a soft spot for him, but where will we put him? The children will be all home for Christmas. I suppose we could manage something…if he really does come … Was he drunk?'

'Yes, of course. Ran out of change, as usual. Cut off. He hasn't

187

been in Ireland for Christmas for decades. Now he's all alone…
Ah! it's probably just a mad drunken spur-of-the-moment idea.'

I was disturbed. I wanted to see my little brother. I still thought
of him like that even though he would be fifty next June. Four
years my junior. I hadn't seen him for years.

***

Life had not given Don the lucky breaks. He was too impatient,
too sensitive, too clever.

Bright as a button in childhood, he was the first to write a story.
I remember him reading it out to us down in the kitchen in
Clontarf.

It was set in New York. It was about the lives of a cop and a
criminal. In the end the baddie is shot dead on the pavement. The
cop turns the body over and cries 'God, it's my brother.'

We all clapped and said eleven-year-old Don should be a writer
when he grew up. As he could have been.

But parental neglect throughout his restless adolescence made
it easy for him to mitch from school after school. Dad promised
him a new bicycle if he stuck it out in his last school, Chanel
College, but he didn't, so instead he was given a one-way ticket for
the boat to England.

At sixteen, he was penniless and alone in London. He signed up
with the British Army, just because 'the nice man offered me a
cigarette and a cup of tea.' He thought Dad would be proud of him
too. He was wrong about that.

In appearance Don looked like a young Tony Curtis – masses
of curly hair, long, long lashes over piercing blue eyes, wry, wide

mouth, and a firm jaw. He was small of stature and had a distinctive deep-throated clipped voice.

He rushed into marriage with a young Irish girl who pursued him back and forth across the Irish Sea, and they had three beautiful children in quick succession. He was a fine soldier, and rose through the ranks, travelling the world, ending up in an army base in Germany.

There was no external war for Don to fight, so his own erupted. He had a lot of spare time, and alcohol was cheap and available in the mess. It helped fill the void at first, then became a necessity. Finally it took priority. His family disintegrated and scattered.

A farewell dinner, a cheque and a briefcase as a parting gift ended Don's army life. He'd served admirably for close on thirty years. He took off for Thailand. He had plans to open an Irish bar there.

When that fell through and his money ran out, he returned to London, and moved in with his younger brother Dermot for a time. He got a job in a sports complex, but as he was in charge of the bar as well, that didn't last too long. He lived with his kind sister and loving daughter for a while, but eventually ended up ill and unemployable in a council flat out near Heathrow.

He rarely saw his family. Vodka and books took their place.

'My pension cheque from the army belongs to my local pub,' he told us, carelessly.

***

When the bell rang and rang at six o'clock in the morning, a few days before Christmas, I should have known who it was.

189

My poor drunken, emaciated wreck of a brother swayed in the porch.

'Di! What kept you? Frank had a heck of a time finding your bloody house!'

As he embraced me in a bear hug, I felt his bones beneath his jacket. The stench of spirits filled the hall.

'Where's everyone?' he roared up the stairs.

'Shush Don, they'll see you soon enough.' I led him into the kitchen.

'Swonderful to be here sis. I did have a bottle of duty-free whiskey for Eamon...but...it's Christmas...and I don't even like whiskey. Now vodka...that's m'baby.'

His once magnificent head of hair was dried, grey and unkempt. His skin had a bluish tinge, and there were gaps in his neglected teeth.

I filled a hot-water bottle and got him up the stairs to take over Paraic's bed, who was getting up for the day.

'Thanks Di...swonderful to be here...talk to you tomorrow.'
'Try to get some sleep. Don. Great to have you here.' But my heart was twisting as I closed the door.

***

On Christmas day we were blessed.

Don had been 'in training', sleeping and drinking milk only. He had stopped vomiting. He appeared thin and shaky, dressed in his best shiny suit.

'I keep it for weddings. I brought it over in my briefcase.'

He was on his best behaviour, charming to all the children, and laughed at the amount of woolly socks he got for presents. He put on his new warm sweater. It helped to stop the shivers. He played around with a side-plate of dinner, then pulled a cracker with gusto.

He stuck to mild drinks until evening.

All the family squashed into the front room for our singsong. With only the glow of the fire and the sparkle of the Christmas tree for light, Don almost looked well. He sang 'Once There Were Green Fields' in his rich deep voice, and won the Elvis impersonating contest with 'Are You Lonesome Tonight?' He easily drank the best part of a bottle of vodka, but still appeared sober.

***

He rang from Dún Laoghaire.

'Best Christmas in living memory!' he roared down the phone. 'And don't worry Di, I won't be making a habit of this.'

He didn't.

He barely hung on through two more Christmases. He died in January – alone – in 'Bangladesh' as he called the area where he lived. I'll always remember him standing against the wall in our front room, beside the tree, surrounded by warmth. And the last line of his song – 'I only know there's nothing left for me, nothing in this wide world left for me to see…'

CALIFORNIA, HERE I COME

Here I am. Dublin Airport. Excited as a five-year-old. Off on my first ever visit to the United States. First time to travel alone. First time to fly in a jumbo jet. I've got all my dollars in a money belt, an outfit for the wedding I'll be attending, and presents for my aunt Helen – who's going to look after me – and who paid for my trip.

Last puff of my pipe with Eamon, Ciarán, and my grandson Joseph, then hugs goodbye.

Head for the duty free. I barely have time to buy a disposable camera and some Irish whiskey.

Served a surprise breakfast aboard the plane – it's Aer Lingus. I've only travelled Ryanair before. Pity I ate a huge meal at home before we left.

Embark at the domestic terminal in Heathrow and walk miles with my heavy bags, and the wedding present. It's a watercolour I painted – a laneway through haystacked fields, montbretia flaming through the greeny banks of County Clare. My son Eoin made the pine frame.

I sneak a final puff of my pipe as I queue for the stand-up bus to the trans-Atlantic terminal.

Fifty minutes later I board the British Airways Boeing to San Francisco. I'm directed through the wide, spacious first class to my seat, and thankfully pack all my gear away in the high locker. But horror – there's no window at my three-tiered row – just a blank, grey tin wall.

I set off to find the chief crewman.

'This is my first flight. I've got to have a window. Please?'

In no time a pleasant stewardess directs me to a windowed row of seats. A young, handsome English couple sit down beside me. I babble on about my trip. They smile politely, then ask if they can move back to my original place. I curl my legs up, explore the little packets of socks, earplugs, eyeshade, blanket. I check my bag for Nicorette, then browse through the menu.

Everything is new and exciting. I'd love a drink.

I wait patiently as I observe the maddeningly slow approach of a young hostess with a tray of drinks. My row at last.

'Would you like red or white wine?' she enquires in a strong Scottish accent.

I've been practicing my answer. 'I'll have both thanks,' I blurt out quickly.

'Pardon?' She doesn't seem to understand me. I repeat my request. She looks baffled.

We smile at each other.

'Are you from Scotland?' I inquire sweetly.

'Yes, I am.'

I lean forward. In my pleasantest voice, I say, very, very, slowly, 'Well…I'm from Ireland. I am speaking English – the same language as yourself – so, if it's all right with you, I'd like to sample both the red and the white wine. Just for a treat.'

We both laugh. Two little bottles are plonked on my tray. *Good Will Hunting* is starting on the big screen, but I give it a miss and, after a delicious dinner of salmon mousse, I snuggle down for a snooze.

I awake to the amazing sight of the Rocky Mountains far down below. The lights inside the cabin are dimmed, and all is quiet as bodies sleep their journey away. Even the crew are missing. Nose pressed against my window, I am hypnotised by the vast, ever-changing sky. The unseen sun glints on an insect-sized plane as it trails towards the horizon.

As we approach San Francisco, I spy Alcatraz and the delicate threads of the Golden Gate Bridge.

I'm sure I can smell fish as I embark.

Deep in the bowels of concrete, I queue for customs. I can't wait to see this 'new world'.

Ground level at last, I greet my two cousins Eileen and Terry, who escort me to his plush, three-rowed station wagon. I admire it while I have a quick puff of my pipe. Thank goodness Terry smokes. Then away from the airport to the nearby Holiday Inn. I see huge cars and trucks, no paths, no one walking. I smell the sea and feel the warmth of the sunshine. It's April, and chilly in Ireland.

Terry has managed to book me into a spacious room, complete with ashtray. 'It's the only smoking room in the hotel,' he assures me. Two giant double beds, a snow-white bathroom. I smoke away, unfettered, and flick through the endless channels on the television. Smiling healthy tanned faces, game shows, *Baywatch*, gospel programmes, soaps. I open my window, say my prayers. I don't know what time it is anymore, I've lost or gained eleven hours somewhere, then I sleep at the edge of a bed that would easily hold five people.

It's light when I wake up. Oh for a cup of tea. I ring reception.

'There's tea and coffee in the room beside reception,' I'm informed.

Luckily I had packed my old dressing gown, so I slip it on and get the lift down. I see a squirrel in the bushes as I cross over to the lobby.

Bright, awake, fully dressed residents pack the tables of a busy breakfast room as I enter.

Startled faces look me over. It's half six by the clock. I try to fill a bowl of cereal from an upside-down glass dispenser, but can't. A Chinese gentleman shows me how to fill two paper cups with coffee. I've no glasses, so I grab a little container that looks like milk. Red-faced, I shuffle back to the safety of my room. I discover I've picked up cream cheese, so drink my coffee black.

In the clinical bathroom, I step in to a low receptacle for a shower, but can't find any knobs. I press all the buttons, but end up having a two-inch bath instead.

Outside at last, in the morning sunshine, Terry waits to drive me to Chico where my aunt lives. From now on, I am completely taken care of – every day mapped out until the wedding.

I compare everything to back home.

In Chico there are magnificent cypress trees, manicured lawns, picket fences. Nobody walks anywhere. Everything works: the air-conditioning, the laundry room, the garage door rises as one approaches by car, the newspapers on the lawn, the sprinklers turn on at exactly the same time each morning.

Everyone wears shorts – even the staff at the airport. No one told me it would be seventy-five degrees in April.

We eat outdoors most of the week, then head up by Sacramento for the wedding itself. Another Holiday Inn, but this one has a swimming pool. Helen lends me her bathing suit, so I swim in the icy pool – all by myself. I sit and admire the palm trees and listen to the housemartins nesting in the eaves of the Mexican-style roof. Then I relax in the small warm tub adjacent. My cousin Eileen joins me. 'Deirdre, why didn't you turn on the Jacuzzi?' I'm grateful it's Eileen and not some stranger who put me wise.

That afternoon my nose and feet get sunburned.

Aunt Helen had expressed a wish for some *céilí* music for the wedding, so that evening I set off down the grass verges along the highway to a music shop I'd noticed earlier. I take a chance and cross the wide, wide road, in a gap of zooming cars. The shop has none of course. Back at the hotel, Helen is aghast. 'You could have been arrested for jay-walking!'

The wedding takes place on a ranch. Enya's 'Orinoco Flow' accompanies the bride and groom as they walk out into the sunshine-flooded veranda, where they are married by a minister. Beneath the hot sun, all the ladies wear short, light summer dresses, with tanned legs and sandals. I am wearing an ankle length navy suit, black tights, and black shoes.

But the champagne is flowing and the food is sumptuous. I meet long-lost relations from County Kerry, who have lived in California for over thirty years, but still retain strong Irish accents.

The newly-weds stay overnight in a ranch-style wooden house, furnished colonial style, with a huge television hidden in an oak wardrobe. I get a lift back to the motel, and sleep like a log in my area of the gigantic bed. Next morning I meet Eileen at breakfast. 'Where did you sleep last night?' I ask. Lots of guests had slept in camper trailers in the grounds outside.

'I slept on the other side of your bed,' she laughs.

Last day.

I'm up early this morning. Half five instead of my usual half six. I shower and pack, then sit in my aunt's peaceful garden, drinking delicious fruit juice, smoking my pipe, saying goodbye to the sunshine, the birds, the wonderful week I've had.

Helen is tired after all the parties, the visitors. She changes the plan to drive me down to San Francisco. 'There's a little aerodrome minutes from here. You can catch a small plane down to the Bay. You'll be there in less than an hour.'

So here I am stepping on to a tiny twelve-seater plane, propellers whirling. Eight bored commuters reading their newspapers. Entranced, I trace the Sacramento River and the tiny swimming pools as we put-put down the coast like a sunstruck bird. I see the Bay, Alcatraz, the ocean, as we circle above San Francisco.

The far-too-young-looking pilot, dressed in shorts, sitting two feet from me, grabs the hand mike, and shouts above the noise of the engines.

'Ladies and gentlemen – there's quite a queue of planes waiting to land. We haven't got enough gas to hang around here all day, so we're going to put you down at Santa Rosa, and a courtesy coach will take you from there.'

Consternation and grumbles from the other passengers. 'I'll miss my connection to Phoenix,' the man beside me groans. But I'm delighted. I've lots of time to spare. Bump, bump, bump, down on concrete again. We're instructed to take our luggage with us. I point to my ten-ton case – bulging with chardonnay wine, presents. 'That's mine over there.' The American airline lady smiles at me. 'Say – you got such a cute accent. Where you from?' I explain. 'Well honey, if you're not in a hurry, you can wait till we refuel then fly on down to the Bay area with us.'

So I have a choice. Delicious. I opt for the coach, as I'll get a close-up look at San Francisco. Across the hilly streets we speed. I think of Steve McQueen's car chase, Judy Garland when the trolleys pass, and earthquakes as we cross the Golden Gate Bridge to the airport.

I get my case taken care of, and then sit outside door number fifty-two, the British Airways' door; there's a myriad of different airlines. I see Chinese coming through the Chinese airlines' door, Africans emerge from the African airlines' door. I drink coffee, enjoy a smoke, soak up the sunshine, observing the elongated limos depositing their passengers at different doors, then glide away silently.

When a plane takes off, the concrete below me bounces – moulded like this for future earthquakes.

I stroll around the horseshoe-shaped airport, then get my hair done in the hairdressing salon. I freshen up in the Ladies – the loo flushes automatically when I stand up!

Have a final puff outside, as I think goodbye. I buy American whiskey and Marlborough cigs in duty free, then dash as the last call is announced for the six o'clock flight to London. I've been here for the past six hours!

Wiser this time, I stretch out on an empty three-seater row at the rear of the plane. It even has a curtain to draw round it. As I pull the blanket over my legs, I notice the cabin crew grinning in my direction.

Oh dear. Apparently it's reserved for them!

Red-faced, I am escorted to the middle row.

Somehow it's Wednesday when we land at Heathrow. I'm sure I left Chico on Monday morning. I've given up working out time zones. I feel squashed in the skinny Aer Lingus plane to Dublin. Handed a Time Out biscuit. Where's my breakfast?

Home to my family – minus my case – it's back in Heathrow. We wait for the presents and the wine, and at seven that evening they are delivered safely by an Aer Lingus van.

The party begins.

'Jet lag? I think it's all in the mind. I feel wonderful!' I tell my children.

Next morning, my body weighs twenty tons. My mind works in slow motion, and my speech follows suit.

She knows. I can see it in her face. 'What are you all doing in my house?' Gráinne manages to strangle out the words, as she walks in the door. Rory, her eldest son, and Roísin, her daughter, encircle her.

'NO!' A deep wail comes from the bottom of her stomach. She bends over double with the pain. I put my arms around her and draw her close. In her anguish she rocks back and forth. 'NO!' she keeps repeating, 'It's not true! It's not true!'

But she knows that it is. Ronán, her charming, gentle, youngest son – barely thirty – has died.

EAMO

A large aluminium teapot, a long wooden ruler, a crammed notebook, and an old-fashioned red telephone with numbered circular holes.

These were the contents of the plastic bag Eamon had plonked on the kitchen table.

The end of his working life.

He had been offered early retirement, and eagerly accepted it. 'That's it, Di. I'm free!'

Eamon had started work in Hely's as an apprentice to the bookbinding trade when he was sixteen. When I met him in the fifties, the printing trade was highly esteemed, well paid and tightly controlled. Nepotism ruled, and Mr Brady had somehow implied that Eamon was related to the Brady who had helped typeset The Proclamation.

Eamon was chuffed to leave school early and to have money in his pocket, but after a fortnight he came home and told his Dad he didn't like working in a factory. 'Nobody likes their job!' was his father's reply.

So Eamon stayed for another forty-five years.

As a youngster he attended St Laurence O'Toole's, and later O'Connell's School. He wasn't very fond of school, but was quite musical. He had (still has) a lovely singing voice, and the music teacher arranged for him to sing at weddings. His Dad sent him for violin lessons, and he could plonk out a tune on the piano by ear.

He also played soccer for North Strand and East Wall. To play for East Wall, a young man had to be a member of the Sodality, and attend their Thursday evening meetings.

'If a chap didn't turn up, the prefect had to call to their house on Saturday to find out why. I had this unenviable job. Now a lot of these were hardchaws – fellows with tough reputations, who'd flatten you in a minute. But they had great respect for their mothers.

I might knock at a house, the mammy would open the door, see me, call her Johnny out, and demand an explanation. "I was down the back of the church. I didn't hear the roll call," was one answer. Naturally I'd say that was fine, "See you for the match."

If Eamon bumped into one of these hardchaws at a dance, or on the road, he knew he had a friend.

But he was no angel himself. He started smoking when he was in short pants. 'I would pinch a few cigarettes from granny's shop, and hide them in the spaces between the stones on the railway wall. I bribed my little brother Joe by giving him one, and we smoked them under the bed!'

When he started working, he handed his wage packet over to his mam every Friday, and she would take so much and give him the rest. He was a snazzy dresser, and wore trendy suits to the weekly hop. He had natural rhythm, and an eye for the girls. The young ladies rather fancied him too.

I remember one night as I waited for the 'ladies' choice' to be announced, a girl sidled up to me and said, 'If you ask Eamon Brady up, I'll bash you. I'm dancing with him!'

Needless to say I allowed her the privilege.

When he and I started to go steady, I looked forward to our Wednesday night visit to the Fairview Cinema. After work I would call to his house, where his mam would give me a huge tea of rashers, egg and chips. Then he would pop into his granny's shop to borrow half a crown from his aunt Tish. He paid it back every Friday, then borrowed it again the next week. One Wednesday evening she declared, in front of the other customers, 'Which one of us owns this half crown?'

As time moved on we were happy together, but now and then I would break it off, as I felt I was too young for commitment. I wasn't sure if my feelings were strong enough to last a lifetime.

But I remember so well the day he came home from hospital after a knee operation. He had been in Jervis Street Hospital for two months. He was thin, pale and very handsome, in a charcoal-grey suit and snow-white shirt and tie. Still on crutches. After the fuss of his family's welcome down in the kitchen, he and I went up to the parlour. He enfolded me in his arms, as I threaded mine around his familiar frame beneath his jacket. We held each other close, without speaking.

I knew then.

A TOUCH OF MIGRAINE

It was that strange Friday, 11 June, when most of Dublin was flooded by the incessant rain. Snug and safe inside my home, I pottered about doing housework, changing all the bed linen, whilst Beethoven's Sixth Symphony – turned up full blast – competed with the thunderous downpour outside. It was quite exciting.

Twelve-year-old Clare and her pal Jenny were having great fun – coming in and out, getting soaked, wading about in the flooded paths and gardens.

I felt grand. I made myself a cup of tea, and sat down in the front room to listen to the final movement.

Suddenly, a sensation similar to a wasp sting exploded inside my skull. I stood up, and felt a burning heat creep up my body, immediately followed by an icy shivering. I fell to my knees and crawled out to the hall, calling out to Clare. I was terrified she wouldn't hear me against the noise of the rain and music. A steel band of pain was now encircling my head, so intense that I couldn't open my eyes.

Vaguely I heard Clare on the telephone beside me.

'Doctor, can you come quickly? I think my mam has fallen down the stairs.'

Jenny ran for my neighbours. I was able to tell them what had happened. Mary, who was a nurse, called an ambulance. Jim, her husband, waited out in the lashings, to make sure it found the right house.

Somehow, the doctor, a stranger Clare had picked out of the

phone book, got through the floods first. He asked me to open my eyes. It was excruciating, but I managed.

'You can send the ambulance away. I'm pretty sure it's a bad migraine. I've given Mrs Brady an injection for the pain.' Then he left.

'I've never had a migraine before,' I moaned to Mary, who held my head and comforted me. Then my kind friends and neighbours carried me into the front room and stayed with me until Eamon arrived at last. He had driven home from work at breakneck speed, up on the paths, through the floods.

At this point there's a blank in my memory of about five days, but my family filled me in on the course of events.

Eamon followed the doctor's instructions. He said I moaned a lot throughout the night but appeared to be sleeping. Early next morning he brought me some food. I didn't know him at all, and my speech was incoherent. He called the ambulance, and Beaumont Hospital doctors quickly diagnosed an aneurysm – a blood vessel had burst in my brain and was bleeding. A scan showed the exact spot. The doctors would have to break open my skull and clip the end of the vein.

It was a terrible time for dear Eamon and the children. Nobody knew how I'd be after surgery.

Each was allowed in to see me before my operation. Fifteen-year-old Máiréad informed me, rather crossly, that I told her to keep up her studies for her Junior Cert. Cailín said, 'You examined the (awful) hospital curtain around your bed, and declared, 'I'm going to get wallpaper just like that!' Ciarán, the eldest, and the joker of the family, recounted the following: 'Ma, you looked at me and you said, "Ciarán, you were always my favourite…all my money is hidden in…" then the nurse said I had to leave!'

My operation was on Sunday evening, but it was not until Tuesday that I became aware of life around me. A nurse was putting cream on my face. Apparently I was black and blue!

'Why are you doing that?' I asked, puzzled.

'You've had major brain surgery.'

Mentally I felt fine. I asked if I could go home the following week as I had to sit my Leaving Cert Art exam. I explained that I was doing one subject per year as a 'mature' student, and this was my last.

An emphatic 'No' was the answer.

However, thanks to the endeavours of my teacher son Eoin, Coláiste Dhúlaigh, the Department of Education and Beaumont Hospital, it was arranged that I could sit my exam in hospital, and I was moved to a room of my own.

The soggy remains of gifts of fruit served for my still life exam, and Joan, my supervisor, posed for my life drawings. She tentatively pointed out that (even though she knew nothing about art), my drawings – depicting a huge head, long body, and short stubby legs, might be slightly out of proportion! We had a good laugh. Naturally, I blamed the medication.

I was allowed to speak into a tape recorder for the History of Art, and Joan listened, enthralled (or so it seemed to me!) as I expounded upon the mysteries of Leonardo's painting of *The Last Supper*, and the intricate architecture and features of the Casino at Marino.

The staff and patients encouraged me warmly, and I made a great recovery. I was discharged after only twelve days, with a c-shaped scar on my half-shaven head.

When I returned for my check-up to my eminent neurosurgeon, I was bursting with questions: Will the clip rust? Could it move? Can I go back to set-dancing classes? He stood up from his desk, raised his hand, palm facing me, to stop my outpourings, and said sternly, 'Well, how did we do? Did we pass the exam?'

CARIBBEAN WAVES

Even up here – far above the Caribbean Sea – standing on Uncle Sean's black marbled floor, the humidity seeps in through the open areas of his huge lounge. There are no windows, no glass, just wooden canopies jutting outside to give some shade. Tropical birds fly in and out as we sip iced Carib beer.

Sean has lived here for over forty years. He is my mother's youngest brother. As a young man, he was sleek and handsome, a charmer and a ladies' man. There are still traces of his good looks in his lanky body, the swaying way he walks, but especially his amazing blue eyes. He speaks in pidgin English with a Trinidadian lilt. He lives here with Brigetta, his third wife, a handsome, blond German lady. He built this house himself – on three levels – clinging to the side of a steeply rising hill overlooking the bay.

Port of Spain, Trinidad, is thirtyish degrees all year round.

'This is why I will never travel back to Ireland. I couldn't stand the cold.'

Sean owns a deep-sea diving and salvage company that he runs mainly over the phone – pacing back and forth, his old leather sandals flapping across the tiles – absent-mindedly stroking his huge dog as he rants and raves about the latest crisis of the current project to whoever is on the other end. He has a secretary, whose open-air 'office' is on the floor below. He rings her throughout the day, keeping track of everything, but I've never seen him actually go down the stairs to talk with her.

Brigetta runs the household quietly and competently – she's a gourmet cook. Every morning she places Sean's breakfast tray (including his tablets) on the table, while he flaps about in his silk dressing gown, arguing loudly on the phone. Every now and then he hollers, 'Where's my glasses?' and we all rush about looking for them.

They have a native Trinidadian woman who comes in to do the cleaning. She sweeps with a slow, languid rhythm, her body moving gracefully across the immense marble floor.

This evening Sean is expansive after dinner. With his drink in one hand he beckons me over to his music centre. I know he loves opera.

'Now, Deirdre, I want you to listen carefully to this. It's from the opera, *Die Tote Stadt*, by Korngold, an Austrian composer. I've put my own words to this aria.'

Seated over in the far corner of the wide lounge, the humid navy sky behind her, Brigitta sighs in a resigned tone, 'Are you sure Deirdre wants to hear it?'

Suddenly, this beautiful room, its curving staircase with copper handrails (salvaged from a ship, Sean told me), red passion flowers scarlet against the black shiny marble floor, is filled with the soaring tones of soprano Katarina Dalayman as she begins the love duet, the 'Lute Song'.

She is Marietta singing of her sad love to Paul.

Sean thrusts a crumpled sheet of paper at me. His rough scribbles have changed the names to Brigitta and Sean, their passionate vows of eternal love rhyme in English. Yet they fit the music perfectly. Sean animatedly sways with the melody – speaks, hums, lives the words, in perfect timing with Paul – ending dramatically with 'This blessed love is ours till the end of time', then signals me for silence as the final notes diminish.

There are tears in my eyes.

Brigitta stands up and enquires, 'Who'd like a drink?'

We are sitting outside our holiday house, on one side of a small sleepy piazza. Basking in the morning sunshine. This is San Pietro in Volta, a tiny fishing village in Pellestrina, a long narrow strip of land adjacent to the famous Lido of Venice. My sisters are staying across the lagoon in Chioggia, as are Terry and Trudi. It's a real working, buzzing town full of character.

A stooped elderly lady sits in her doorway just down from us, expertly weaving fine, cream lace. A small child wobbles through the piazza on her scooter. We smile at her, say 'Buongiorno.'

We half read our books, drink mugs of tea, chat lazily now and then, enjoy our smokes.

A young man we've met before, who speaks a little English, walks slowly past us. He has a wad of Italian newspapers under his arm. A huge photo on the front page catches our attention. As I crane my neck to look closer, he shows it to us.

It is the twin towers in New York – blazing with filthy smoke and debris.

It had happened yesterday. We knew nothing about it until this moment.

Today is 12 September 2001.

DERMOT

Twenty-ninth of February, 2004. My youngest brother died today at a quarter past two.

They did everything they could for him in the Intensive Care Unit of the Mater Hospital, and treated him with such dignity. We went back in to see him for the last time. No machines. Clean sheets, a fresh, pink blanket covering Dermot. The bloated appearance gone. His face more aquiline, a creamy white now. Black neat eyebrows, eyes completely closed, mouth slightly open. His hair brushed and curling at his neck.

Marian's bunch of spring flowers and Niamh's photo of him (doubled up, laughing, white swans on the river behind him) in a basket above his head. Our medal from Fatima placed on his chest.

I thought of the words the English chaplain had spoken just before he died.

Leaning over the bed, up close to Dermot, he had placed a hand firmly on his forehead, all the time looking directly at his immobile face. Then, slowly and clearly, he said, 'Now Dermot, I am going to give you a special blessing. Your family are here with you too. I absolve you from all your past sins. You can take your leave now, and not be afraid. Goodbye, and may God speed you safely on your way.'

Then Dermot faded silently away from us.

***

The council flat where Dermot used to live was situated just far enough from the centre of historic Chester to ensure he had no visitors. It suited him. He guarded his privacy. He preferred to drink his cans and his cider there, and shied away from pubs.

His health was poor and he existed on disability money and help from two sisters in particular.

They looked out for him all the years he lived in England and Wales.

When Nuala's book was successful, she decided that it was time Dermot returned to Dublin – to be near us – his sisters and families, so she bought him a solid little house near Fairview. He was not unduly excited about this, but he quit Chester without a backward glance. He had one good friend, Den, who kept in touch.

Dermot had been away for over thirty years.

In the beginning he referred to his new home as 'Nuala's', and took little interest in it. He spent his time going through the tangle of forms, appointments, phone calls necessary to obtain a disability allowance and medical card. In and out of hospital too.

He visited Gráinne and me weekly. He came to our house every Sunday. Most of the children and grandchildren came for Eamon's dinner.

At first he was polite and convivial, a stranger to them and almost to me too.

The little ones kept their distance from this strange fellow hunched over in the corner of the sofa – wrapped in layers of old jumpers and a scarf, rolling his tobacco, waving his hand in the air every now and then saying 'Don't fuss!' or 'Whatever'. His blotchy complexion, and whistle of air every time he spoke (he had a tube in his throat from a long spell in hospital) didn't help either.

I only knew snatches of his life. Having quit the hostel where Mammy had left him when he was barely sixteen, he had lived for a time in squats, had some girl friends, and had worked as a postman in London, where he had secured his own flat.

Even though he'd shoved the 'problem of Dermot' across the sea, Dad organised a big twenty-first for him. All his brothers and sisters travelled to the celebrations in a swanky hotel in London. Dermot was then a good-looking young man, always thin, with long abundant black curly hair, and slightly protruding, big dark eyes.

His whole life ahead of him.

But when he and one lady got together, his life took a turn for the worse. They were bad for each other. Both had drinking problems, and the fights became worse and worse. They separated, and poor, damaged, addicted Dermot ended up living alone in Chester.

Back in Dublin, Dermot's health continued to deteriorate, and he was in and out of hospital for long spells. Gradually he began to get to know us, and to believe that his house was really his own home. He proudly nurtured a few plants placed around his all-important television. It was his companion through the long uneventful days.

His neighbours, especially Rosaleen, were kind, caring, non-judgemental. They all knew he drank. Rosaleen gave him net curtains, a suite of furniture and a dressing gown when he was hospitalised. Theresa, his home help, became a friend to him. Just like in Chester, he didn't like callers, but Theresa was an exception.

Neither Gráinne or I would dream of calling without phoning first.

As his time was running out, Nurse Maura called on him regularly. 'She would bang on that door until Dermot answered her, to make sure he was all right,' Rosaleen told me.

We were no longer on tenterhooks when Dermot strolled in on Sunday afternoons. Everyone was used to his odd ways by now. Sometimes he would bring a battered rose wrapped in newspaper from the wild bush that grew under his front window. He was comfortable enough with the children to shout 'Shut the bloody door, will you?' when they raced in and out of dining room. He got on really well with Cailín, Clare and Máiréad, and shared stories with them about some of his London exploits in his younger years.

One Sunday, as our gang talked noisily around the kitchen table, Dermot sat on the sofa, mug of wine in hand, staring into space.

Two-year-old Ellie toddled over to him, a ladybird book in her hand. She plonked it on his knees and looked steadily at him. 'All right. you win... I will read it to you,' he affected a pained tone. She climbed on to his lap, smiled up at his poor ravaged face, and nestled happily against his chest as he read *Snow White* in his slow, hesitant way.

Little Aunt Anne, ninety-one years and three months old, our last link to our childhood, and the past of Mam and Dad.

Anne is as bright as a button mentally, but her brave little heart is giving out.

The nurses are kind as could be – the radio is on low in her room, and Roísín's sweet pea are on the window ledge. Anne is propped up, eyes closed. She is wearing pink-spotted pyjamas, and has pushed back the covers. We can see her tiny pigeon chest rising and falling laboriously.

As I take her thin speckled hand in mine, she opens her fading eyes and looks at Gráinne. 'I'm dying,' she manages to mouth, then repeats, 'I'm dying.' We can see that she is frightened.

'Don't fret Anne – you've been a great aunt to us all the years – you never did anything bad in your whole life.'

She nods her head.

'We don't want to tire you – have a little rest – then we'll come back again.'

As we stand to leave, with a huge effort, Anne whispers, slowly and clearly, 'I love you Gráinne… I love you Deirdre.'

A DIP IN THE SEA

On Sunday, 11 July 2004, four brothers from Dublin arrived at the coast of Dover. Their goal was to swim the channel between there and France as a relay team. If they succeeded, they would be the first-ever Irish team of brothers to achieve this record.

They were Ciarán, 40; Paraic, 38; Eoin, 36; and Dónal, 29.

Point-to-point, the distance between Dover and Cap Gris-Nez in France is twenty-two and a half miles, but most swims are nearer the thirty-mile mark because you can't just travel in a straight line and you have to allow for winds, tides, currents and ships.

Paraic, the most experienced swimmer, had trained to swim the channel solo the previous summer, but he was denied his chance by bad weather. However, his boat was still booked, so throughout the winter months the boys decided they'd try a relay swim instead because relay teams are allowed to chance the crossing in less than favourable weather. So, they began to train in the swimming pool, and later in the Irish Sea.

They also agreed to publicise their swim to raise money for Our Lady's Hospital for Sick Children in Crumlin.

They were given a window of one week by the Channel Swimming and Pilot Federation – 10 to 17 July.

Not just anybody can take off and attempt the crossing. There are all sorts of rules and regulations. Each person must have a medical, and have completed several hours swimming in the sea. A recognised skipper must pilot the boat that accompanies the swimmers. He must know the tides, currents, shipping lanes – over

500 large ships and ferries use that stretch of water every day. An official from the federation has to be on board to make sure all rules are adhered to. Swimmers may only wear ordinary bathing suits, goggles and hat; no such thing as a wet suit. They are allowed to smear grease or Vaseline on their bodies.

Someone has to watch out for the swimmers in case of jellyfish, seals, hypothermia, sickness, and fatigue. They also have to make sure the swimmer does not stray too far or too close to the boat. Drinks are thrown down, usually hot tea, in a special container. If a swimmer touches the boat at any time, he or she is disqualified. When a swim takes place in darkness, a light has to be fitted to the back of the togs.

The Irish team arrived at their caravan site on Sunday night. This is where Channel swimmers from all over the world stay, overlooking the white cliffs of Dover.

The boys met people from Germany, USA, Australia, and a young Malaysian man who was studying in Cambridge, all waiting for their chance. Each had been given a time slot to make their attempt, each with their own approved pilot and boat.

The brothers were next on the list.

All their preparation behind them, they settled down to wait for the go-ahead. They had a bagful of energy food and drinks, warm jackets (they had borrowed sister Máiréad's ski jacket), hats, gloves, track bottoms. With them was their father, Eamon, and Aran, their cousin, who flew especially from Colorado. Their highly important job would be to watch the swimmers, shout encouragement and time splits. Ciarán's son Joseph, aged ten years, had come as well for the adventure.

Sunday, the weather was cold and rainy. The skipper told them that Monday was too windy to chance it. Tuesday looked promising, so their hopes were high.

Monday night they got word. Be down at the boat at seven o'clock the next day. Eamon made a hearty stew for all – the last proper meal anyone of them would have for the next twenty-four hours. They all bedded down early, but got very little sleep.

Next morning they met their pilot – a cheerful Cockney called Eddie Spelling who called everyone 'Me Mucker'. He gave the boys a few tips. 'Channel grease won't really protect you from the cold water, but it helps to prevent chaffing. The skin can get sore and raw as you constantly graze your chin against your shoulders with each stroke.'

He took them out of the harbour, where the huge ships berthed, and around to Shakespeare's Bay. On deck, the family linked arms in a circle, bowed their heads, and said a prayer that God would watch over them.

Paraic was to do the first hour. He dived from the boat and swam in to the beach. As soon as he landed on English sand, he turned and raised his two hands in the air. At exactly 8.31 a.m., the official siren was sounded. He plunged into the water and set off in the direction of France. The weather was cool, but sunny, and the sea was fairly calm. He swam strongly and speedily alongside the boat. 'Never swim behind it,' he had advised the others. 'The ladder looks too tempting when you're exhausted and cold.'

One hour later, Eoin dived in alongside Paraic and moved past him. Only then could Paraic board the boat. Not a bother on him. Eoin covered a lot of sea in his hour, and emerged, shivering and cold, but intact. Next in was Ciarán. He too felt the cold and swam as fast as he could to keep the circulation going. Eoin and Ciarán are very thin, and a girth of flesh is the best protection from prolonged immersion in the sea. Paraic, who carries a bit of extra fat, said 'It's the first time my skinny brothers were envious of my generous figure!'

Finally it was Dónal's turn, the youngest brother, who had only returned from Uganda two days before, and had not been able to train in the sea with the others. But he did his stint, keeping up an even pace.

On they battled throughout the day. About seven miles from the coast of France, the wind suddenly strengthened, and the sea whipped up choppy waves. Joseph and the official observer were seasick as the boat swayed and bucked. As soon as Eoin boarded, he too was sick, but it was when Ciarán climbed out of the water that Eamon and Aran thought the swim might have to be aborted.

He was blue all over, and passed out. The boys rubbed his body, dressed him in warm clothes, gave him hot tea, and squeezed in beside him, trying to give him warmth. Eddie brought up tin foil to wrap around Ciarán. 'Watch his lips don't turn blue,' he warned, as he started down the steps again. Turning to Eamon and Aran he added, in a dry tone, 'That's knocked the b****x out of him anyway!'

The rest of the team pressed on. France was tantalisingly close. By the time it was his turn again, Ciarán had recovered. 'France, here we come. No problem!' he shouted into the wind.

Some way out at sea, the pilot stopped his engines. 'I can't go any closer. There are rocks and underwater spikes. It's too dangerous.'

The official observer gave the boys their instructions. 'The next man has to swim to the shore of Cap Gris-Nez, stand up, raise his arms in the air, then swim back to the boat.'

Everyone gathered up on deck. Nobody spoke as they watched Paraic thread the dark water. Thirty-one seconds after nine o'clock, just as dusk was setting, he stood up on French sand. There was a huge roar from the boat.

It had taken them exactly twelve hours, twenty-nine minutes and thirty one seconds – an excellent time. They would be in the record books. They had achieved their dream.

The Brady bunch had made it!

A QUIET BREAK

I had made it clear to Eamon, 'I'd just like a nice rest – me and you – for my birthday. No fuss, no surprise party.'

He booked this weekend for us in the Ballymascanlon Hotel. We arrived late yesterday after a nightmare crawl through traffic near Drogheda. As I admired our room in the new wing, Eamon suggested casually, 'How would you like to go out for dinner? There's a nice restaurant up the road.'

I was not enthusiastic. 'We've only just arrived!' But I agreed.

Off out the road again. The waitress enquired, 'Table for two? This way please.'

She ushered us in to a large room – three tables butted together at the far end. Strange.

Suddenly the room erupted with cries of 'Happy Birthday!' and, from beneath the tablecloths, the darling faces of my children, their partners, husbands, wives, and my grandchildren, popped up. Only Dónal was missing. He was in Australia.

It took months of organising, planning, telling fibs, getting off work, timing, so that they would all be there before me.

**

The screams, shouts, noise and laughter are hitting off the glass roof of the hotel swimming pool. I sit and watch as they all splash, swim and cavort. Six-month-old baby Ellie sits on my lap, fascinated by the antics of the familiar faces she knows.

Last night at dinner Ciarán presented me with my present. Bits and pieces of my life bound in a slim book – all prepared secretly with Eamon's help.

My family are taking up the entire pool. They shout, 'Look at me Nana, I can swim!' or 'Mam, watch this dive' or 'Deirdre, are you all right?'

I smile and nod at them all. The morning sun is slanting through the floor length windows. I can see the carefully manicured lawn, the majestic blue-green alpine trees.

Right this moment I am perfectly fine.